# New Daylight

Edited by Naomi Starkey                    September–December 2008

GW00371289

# Suggestions for using *New Daylight*

Find a regular time and place, if possible, where you can read and pray undisturbed. Before you begin, take time to be still and perhaps use the BRF prayer. Then read the Bible passage slowly (try reading it aloud if you find it over-familiar), followed by the comment. You can also use *New Daylight* for group study and discussion, if you prefer.

The prayer or point for reflection can be a starting point for your own meditation and prayer. Many people like to keep a journal to record their thoughts about a Bible passage and items for prayer. In *New Daylight* we also note the Sundays and special festivals from the Church calendar, to keep in step with the Christian year.

# *New Daylight* and the Bible

*New Daylight* contributors use a range of Bible versions, and you will find a list of the versions used in each issue at the back of the notes on page 154. You are welcome to use your own preferred version alongside the passage printed in the notes, and this can be particularly helpful if the Bible text has been abridged.

*New Daylight* affirms that the whole of the Bible is God's revelation to us, and we should read, reflect on and learn from every part of both Old and New Testaments. Usually the printed comment presents a straight-forward 'thought for the day', but sometimes it may also raise questions rather than simply providing answers, as we wrestle with some of the more difficult passages of Scripture.

New Daylight *is also available in a deluxe edition (larger format). Check out your local Christian bookshop or contact the BRF office, who can also give more details about a cassette version for the visually impaired. For a Braille edition, contact St John's Guild, 8 St Raphael's Court, Avenue Road, St Albans, AL1 3EH.*

# Writers in this issue

**Naomi Starkey** is the Editor of *New Daylight*. She also edits *Quiet Spaces*, BRF's prayer and spirituality journal, as well as commissioning BRF's range of books for adults.

**John Proctor** is married to Elaine, with an adult daughter and son. He works for the United Reformed Church in Cambridge as a teacher of the New Testament. John has written *The People's Bible Commentary: Matthew* (BRF, 2001) and booklets on the Gospels in the Grove Biblical Series.

**Veronica Zundel** is an Oxford graduate, writer and journalist. She lives with her husband and young son in North London, where they belong to the Mennonite Church.

**David Robertson** has ministered in a variety of parishes since his ordination in 1979 and is currently a vicar in Halifax. He has written *Marriage—Restoring Our Vision* and *Collaborative Ministry* for BRF.

**Helen Julian CSF** is an Anglican Franciscan sister, currently serving her community as Minister Provincial. She has written *Living the Gospel* and *The Road to Emmaus* for BRF.

**Stephen Rand** is a writer and speaker who in recent years has shared his time between Jubilee Debt Campaign, persecuted church charity Open Doors, and Mainstream, a Baptist church leaders' network. Stephen is the author of *When the Time Was Right*, a BRF book of Advent readings.

**Stephen Cottrell** is the Bishop of Reading. He has worked in parishes in London and Chichester, as Pastor of Peterborough Cathedral, as Missioner in the Wakefield diocese and as part of Springboard, the Archbishop's evangelism team. He has written widely about evangelism and spirituality; his latest books are *From the Abundance of the Heart* (DLT, 2006) and *Do Nothing to Change Your Life* (CHP, 2007).

**Adrian Plass** is an internationally popular writer and speaker in many countries. His most recent books for BRF are *When You Walk* (revised and expanded) and *Blind Spots in the Bible*.

**Tony Horsfall** is a freelance trainer and associate of EQUIP, a missions programme based at Bawtry Hall near Doncaster. He is an elder of his local church in West Yorkshire, and regularly travels abroad leading retreats and Quiet Days. His latest book for BRF is *Mentoring for Spiritual Growth*.

For more in-depth coverage of some of the passages in these
Bible reading notes, we recommend the following titles:

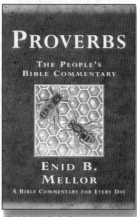

978 1 84101 071 7, £7.99

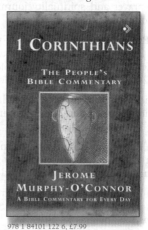

978 1 84101 122 6, £7.99

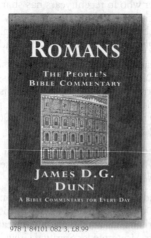

978 1 84101 082 3, £8.99

978 1 84101 066 3, £8.99

# Naomi Starkey writes...

In this September to December issue, I am delighted to welcome Bishop Stephen Cottrell as a contributor. He has previously worked with BRF as an author, producing *On This Rock* (2003) and, just this year, *The Adventures of Naughty Nora*, a book of fun stories for use in schools, published under BRF's *Barnabas* imprint. He has now written on 'Words of challenge and consolation' for *New Daylight*.

Also in this issue we cover the concluding part of Paul's letter to the Romans, with the help of John Proctor, while Helen Julian brings us another instalment from the book of Exodus (chapters 15—19). Adrian Plass gets to grips with some proverbs, while Veronica Zundel shares thoughts on sin and salvation—two enormous themes that are central to the Christian story, yet often misunderstood by the wider world.

Continuing our readings in 1 Corinthians, we have Stephen Rand as our guide through chapters 5 to 8. His title aptly sums up the flavour of these Bible passages—'Not in front of the children'—but, while not everybody may like what Paul has to say, it is important that we read and reflect on such teaching, as part of our growth as disciples. Given the fact that *New Daylight* operates on a page-a-day format, it is impossible to answer all the questions raised as thoroughly as some may wish, but that does not mean that we cannot ask the questions and, in so doing, begin a process of healthy debate.

Concluding *New Daylight* for 2008, Tony Horsfall writes on 'Christmas words'. Although the Bible stories we hear at this time of year may be very familiar, and we may wonder how to recapture something of their original drama and mystery, we can pray that God will speak to us afresh as we reflect on the child, the birth, the angels, the joy and the wonder.

And here's something to look forward to in the New Year: from time to time, readers have written to request that we include introductions for every set of readings. In the past we have not been able to manage this, due to lack of space, but from the next issue we shall be slimming down the Magazine section by a few pages. This gives us enough room to ensure that whenever a new contributor starts his or her section, a full introduction is provided.

# The BRF Prayer

*Almighty God,*
*you have taught us that your word is a lamp for our feet*
*and a light for our path. Help us, and all who prayerfully*
*read your word, to deepen our fellowship with each other*
*through your love. And in so doing may we come to know you*
*more fully, love you more truly, and follow more faithfully in*
*the steps of your son Jesus Christ, who lives and reigns with*
*you and the Holy Spirit, one God for evermore. Amen.*

# Free feast

'Come, all you who are thirsty, come to the waters; and you who have no money, come, buy and eat! Come, buy wine and milk without money and without cost. Why spend money on what is not bread, and your labour on what does not satisfy? Listen, listen to me, and eat what is good, and you will delight in the richest of fare.'

To us this passage may sound like a glorified *Supermarket Sweep*, where lucky punters dash down the aisles and stuff as much food as possible into their trolleys. In a culture dominated by subsistence farming, however, where the 'sweat of your brow' (Genesis 3:19) determined how much you and your community had to eat, this passage would have been jaw-droppingly astonishing. I have tried and failed to look after an allotment. As a result I feel that I have an—admittedly minuscule—insight into how much sheer hard work is involved in growing your own food. I have imagined what it must have been like in times past (and in other countries today) to have to work like that season after season after season—or starve.

God is calling out to his people—the nation of Israel, exiled in Babylon—promising them the most lavish of feasts, all completely free. It is an invitation to share in the abundant life that he longs to give them—the 'wine and milk... bread... the richest of fare'

symbolizing the spiritual blessings that he is desperate to lavish on them. Even the poorest of the poor are welcome and they will eat as well as the wealthiest family.

We can become so focused on the fact of our fallen state, how we need to receive forgiveness for our sins before our relationship with God can be restored, that we forget to reflect on his astonishing generosity. We can remember that 'all have sinned and fallen short of the glory of God' (Romans 3:23), yet overlook the very next verse: 'and all are justified freely by his grace through the redemption that came by Christ Jesus.' The key word here is 'freely'—he gives and asks for nothing in return but that we accept the gift.

### Prayer

*Thank you, generous Lord, that your heart's desire is to give us more than we could imagine or ask for. May we be ready to receive from you.*

NS

# Reaching the nations

'Give ear and come to me; listen, that you may live. I will make an everlasting covenant with you, my faithful love promised to David. See, I have made him a witness to the peoples, a ruler and commander of the peoples. Surely you will summon nations you know not, and nations you do not know will come running to you, because of the Lord your God, the Holy One of Israel, for he has endowed you with splendour.'

This passage tells us that yesterday's promised food fest is more than a charity lunch for all and sundry. Our invitation is to a family meal—not as one-off guests, but as relatives. God the Father, the banquet's host, requests the pleasure of our company, not only sitting at his table but also coming to live in his heavenly home as his covenant children.

Accepting the invitation, and the exalted position of being members of God's family, means that we are given the privilege of work to do. Like David, chosen to be king and to be 'a ruler and commander of the peoples', the people of Israel were called to be a witness to the glory of God. Like Jesus himself, hailed as the Son of David, their task was to make 'the Holy One of Israel' known to all nations.

This is an extension of God's original promise to David (and to those before him), not a brand new arrangement. The whole nation is being summoned to serve God's purpose, which is nothing less than reaching out to those outside the covenant: 'nations you do not know… will come running to you', captivated by the glory shining around the children of the King of kings.

In this passage we can hear echoes, too, of the Magi coming from 'the east' to worship the child Jesus (Matthew 2:1–12) and John's vision of the vast throng worshipping before God's throne, 'from every nation, tribe, people and language' (Revelation 7:9). As the course of history unfolds, the Father will continue to seek ways in which to draw his beloved, wayward creatures back to himself.

**Prayer**

*Grant us a vision, heavenly Father, of the wideness of your mercy and the breadth of your love. May we, your children, be known by the marks of your character we bear.*

NS

# Moment of opportunity

'Seek the Lord while he may be found; call on him while he is near. Let the wicked forsake their ways and the unrighteous their thoughts. Let them turn to the Lord, and he will have mercy on them, and to our God, for he will freely pardon.'

The ancient Greek word *kairos* meant 'the right or opportune moment', a time of special significance, and there is a sense of this meaning in our passage today. God is close at hand and wants to speak to us, but are we ready to hear?

Throughout the Bible we find promises that, if we seek God, we will find him, if we seek 'with all [our] heart' (see Jeremiah 29:13–14; also Deuteronomy 4:29, Matthew 6:33, Hebrews 11:6 and elsewhere). If we ignore his call, mentally park it to respond to at a less busy time, we may find that it grows increasingly faint amid the noise of daily life.

As Jesus walked through the Galilean countryside, huge crowds flocked to hear his teaching and seek healing. While some chose to join his disciples, there must have been many who simply followed him around for a while and then lost interest when something more pressing—or more immediately gratifying—turned up. They certainly heard the Master's voice, but then stopped paying attention and wandered off.

If we recognize ourselves as being among those who always seem to find an excuse for putting off spending time in the Lord's presence, we shouldn't lash ourselves in a guilt-stricken frenzy. It's too easy to get into a cycle of guilt about not reading our Bible/praying and then starting to loathe the very thought of it because that induces more guilt and it becomes easier to forget about it instead. I know—I've done it many times.

The verses above speak of free pardon. God longs for us to come to him, like a parent longing for a moody teenager to come and share something about their day. He won't turn away coldly when we approach because we haven't come earlier, but, like the father in the parable of the runaway son (Luke 15:11–32), will rush towards us, arms open, to embrace us.

### Prayer

*Thank you, Father, that you love our company, long for us to turn back to you and will forgive all our frailties and failings.*

NS

# Higher than the heavens

'For my thoughts are not your thoughts, neither are your ways my ways,' declares the Lord. 'As the heavens are higher than the earth, so are my ways higher than your ways and my thoughts than your thoughts.'

Richard Wurmbrand, the late Romanian pastor and campaigner for the persecuted Church, spent 14 years in prison under the former communist regime. He told of how his atheist persecutors mocked him for continuing to believe in God even though space exploration had revealed no trace of a divine presence beyond the sky. 'That proves nothing,' was his reply. 'An ant could walk around my boot and say that it had seen no trace of Wurmbrand.'

Our verses today are a reminder that God—by definition—exists on an unimaginably different scale from that of his finite creation. Isaiah 40:22 speaks of God sitting 'enthroned above the circle of the earth' and, by comparison, 'people are like grasshoppers'. That is a poetic image, of course. God is not literally up in the sky, watching us from a fluffy white cloud. What it does point out, however, is that, while he is certainly gracious, patient and loving, he is also the Lord Almighty, present and complete in himself from before the beginning, everlasting to everlasting.

The concluding chapters of the book of Job make this same point at much greater length. Job and his friends have spent hours agonizing (literally, in Job's case) over the mystery of suffering. Today's social and therapeutic niceties might lead us to expect God to respond, 'I hear what you're saying, I hear your anger; you seem to find all this hard to understand. Well, let me reassure you…'

Instead, he simply says, in effect, 'Who are you to presume to question me? Have you forgotten who I am?' In verses of breathtaking poetry, we are reminded of God's majesty and creative power. We may be made in his image, but we are still creatures, not the Creator. Our minds cannot begin to contain all that he knows.

### Reflection

*In Eden, man and woman grasped for the 'knowledge of good and evil' when God forbade them to do so (Genesis 2:17). Who knows with what wisdom and insight he would have blessed them, had they waited for him to bring them to maturity?*

*NS*

# God's purposes

'As the rain and the snow come down from heaven, and do not return to it without watering the earth and making it bud and flourish, so that it yields seed for the sower and bread for the eater, so is my word that goes out from my mouth: it will not return to me empty, but will accomplish what I desire and achieve the purpose for which I sent it.'

My younger son is going through a dinosaur phase and, this being the second time I have had an amateur palaeontologist in the house, I have become well acquainted with some of those astonishing creatures. Even so, my mind still boggles at quite how long ago they lived. When you start to explore the world of rocks and minerals, you discover the brain-expanding scope of geological time.

It is easy for us to assume that our planet is, as a matter of course, centred on the human race. We think that it is all about us, all the time. Yes, we are made in the image of God, but it seldom occurs to us that we are just one small part of an unfolding cosmic plan.

Today's verses remind us of *God's* perspective. In the words of Arthur Ainger's hymn, God is working his purpose out, as year succeeds to year, and the fulfilment of God's plans is as inevitable as the fact that rainfall produces plant growth, with the resulting benefits for farmer and consumer.

We find another reminder of this passage (and the hymn) in Habakkuk 2:13–14: 'Has not the Lord Almighty determined that the people's labour is only fuel for the fire, that the nations exhaust themselves for nothing? For the earth will be filled with the knowledge of the glory of the Lord as the waters cover the sea.' Note that here it is the *knowledge* of the glory of the Lord—we're not just talking an invisible divine presence or a subtle glow. One day, all eyes will see and acknowledge that the Lord, Yahweh, is God.

We may feel like we are stuck in a hard place, that we can do nothing worthwhile to bring the kingdom of heaven to earth, yet of one thing we can be sure: God—Father, Son, Spirit—is at work behind the scenes.

**Prayer**

*Thank you, Lord, that nothing can thwart your purposes.*

NS

# Creation celebration

'You will go out in joy and be led forth in peace; the mountains and hills will burst into song before you, and all the trees of the field will clap their hands. Instead of the thorn bush will grow the juniper, and instead of briars the myrtle will grow. This will be for the Lord's renown, for an everlasting sign, that will endure for ever.'

The jubilation here resonates with echoes from elsewhere in scripture. Surely the juniper and myrtle replacing the thorny scrub reverses the curse laid on the soil after the Fall: 'Cursed is the ground because of you… It will produce thorns and thistles for you' (Genesis 3:17–18). The people here are being 'led forth in peace'—much better than their horrific experience of being led into exile—but we also catch a reminder of the exodus when they were led from slavery to freedom and a promised land flowing with good things. In the joy of this glorious return, the land itself bursts into praise.

It is the language of poetry, but it can also serve as a reminder that God sees us as being intricately linked to the world he created for us. It is not just a stage for our actions, but our home, which we are called to cherish. As many have come to realize, sustainable living is a biblical imperative. So, would our land rejoice at the prospect of our return or heave a sigh of relief to see the back of us? Hold on to that thought.

In this week's readings, we have been reminded how the Lord Almighty, maker of heaven and earth, loves us and longs to return to the intimacy he enjoyed with humankind in Eden. If we accept the offer of relationship that he holds out and the responsibilities that come with it, we will be blessed with the certain hope that one day we will live with him in a great city, made beautiful with a river and trees that offer life and healing to the nations, who have come at last to share in his eternal feast.

### Reflection

*'And I heard a loud voice from the throne saying, "Look! God's dwelling place is now among people, and he will dwell with them. They will be his people, and God himself will be with them and be their God"' (Revelation 21:3).*

NS

# Romans 9—16

Starting Romans at chapter 9 is like turning on the television midway through a major news item. You hear reactions to what has happened. People are explaining how it affects the way we view the world and how we should respond, but you have missed what was said about the incident itself.

The great event, so far as Romans is concerned, was the cross and resurrection of Jesus. God's Son has died for sinners and God has raised him from the dead. Love is linked to power, sacrifice to victory, pardon to hope and heaven to earth. Paul explains all of this in the first half of his letter. He bubbles over with enthusiasm and conviction as he outlines what God has done for the world.

Then, in the second half of Romans, we start to see some of the burdens Paul carried and the pastoral concerns that arose from his faith in Jesus. First, we see how passionately Paul cared for the Jewish nation, to which he belonged himself. Only a minority of their people had welcomed the message of Jesus as Messiah. Paul was pained by this and, in chapters 9 to 11, he explores what it might mean, as part of God's long-standing relationship with Israel.

In chapters 12 and 13, he turns to the church in Rome, the people who would hear his letter read aloud to them. They were a small group in a big city, a new religious movement in a land with a strong sense of history. They would need commitment, unity and wisdom as they lived the Christian life among their neighbours.

Finally, in the last chapters, Paul opens up an issue that concerned him deeply. The Christian community in Rome was a mixed company. Some were Jewish by race, others were Gentiles (this word simply means non-Jewish). With big differences in culture and background to overcome, it was hard for Christians from the two groups to feel as if they were one family in Christ.

Paul, however, believed that Christians belong together and we should take our commitment to each other seriously. The love we owe each other as Christians expresses the love God has given us in Christ. The fellowship we find in the Church grows out of the faith we share in the Christian gospel, which tells of God's greatest deeds—the death and resurrection of Jesus.

*John Proctor*

# Plaque and passion

I have great sorrow and unceasing anguish in my heart. For I could wish that I myself were accursed and cut off from Christ for the sake of my own people, my kindred according to the flesh. They are Israelites, and to them belong the adoption, the glory, the covenants, the giving of the law, the worship, and the promises; to them belong the patriarchs, and from them, according to the flesh, comes the Messiah.

Some houses in Britain have a blue plaque on the wall, to record the fact that a famous person once lived there. This, we read, was the birthplace or workshop or family home of someone whose name we know from the history books or their public life. Paul's point in today's verses is that the history of Israel has a blue plaque on it. Jesus came from there.

Out of Israel's story God brought the good news of the gospel. What God did through the long years of the Old Testament, the relationship he forged with Israel, the ways that he blessed and guided them, their testimony of faith and praise—all that was vital. It was an era of preparation, making ready for the coming of Jesus the Messiah.

Yet Paul found that many Israelite people, those he looked on as his natural family, had not welcomed the message about Jesus. Many did not look on Jesus as a true Messiah. For Paul this was agonizingly sad. He saw so much potential and blessing in Israel's past, yet many of her people had not recognized the fulfilment of that potential in Jesus.

Paul was not angry with those Jewish people who did not share his faith—he wanted to love them. He would do anything, he says, to bring them to Jesus Christ. If he could, he would even trade his own relationship with God, for their sake.

In a way, that is what Jesus did on the cross: entering the darkness of separation from God, for the sake of others. No one else can do that and no one else needs to, but it is still right to care. Like Paul, we may feel passion and pain when we pray that others, even our family or closest friends, will come to faith.

### Prayer

*Lord, please use my prayers and my life to help others know your love.*

JP

# Narrow line of promise

It is not as though the word of God had failed. For not all Israelites truly belong to Israel, and not all of Abraham's children are his true descendants; but 'It is through Isaac that descendants shall be named after you.' This means that it is not the children of the flesh who are the children of God, but the children of the promise are counted as descendants.

Paul looks back into history as he tries to understand God's work in Israel. He realizes that God has often concentrated on a narrow line within the nation. The story of Israel was a waiting and sifting process. God was nurturing faith, rather than working automatically through genes and family trees.

At the start of Israel's story, Abraham had two sons and the younger son, Isaac, was the one who carried the promise. His birth had been promised, when nature itself seemed to rule it out as Sarah and Abraham were too old to have children. So, from the cradle, Isaac was a son of faith, whereas the older son, Ishmael, born of Sarah's maidservant Hagar, was a 'child of the flesh'. He had Abraham's genes, but faith and promise were not part of his story in the same way that they were part of Isaac's.

This sort of process happened time and again, says Paul. At times of change and crisis, there was an Israel emerging within Israel, a narrow line of faith and hope to carry God's covenant forward. God's ways were consistent through the years and God never gave up. There was always a 'remnant' (v. 27), to sustain the faith into the future.

I wonder if some of Paul's readers wondered why God acted so mysteriously. Similar questions may arise for us. How should we expect God to work today, in our families or local churches? How does God's purpose go forward, from one generation to another? I think Paul might say that grace is always reliable, but not always predictable. You cannot tell exactly what God will do next. When we are led by unexpected or perplexing ways, that does not mean God has forgotten or his word has fallen dead. We still have cause to wait and trust.

### Prayer

*God of wisdom, when I cannot understand everything you do, help me to trust in the truth you have already taught me and the love you have given.*

JP

# Wide purpose of love

What if God, desiring to show his wrath and to make known his power, has endured with much patience the objects of wrath that are made for destruction; and what if he has done so in order to make known the riches of his glory for the objects of mercy, which he has prepared beforehand for glory—including us whom he has called, not from the Jews only but also from the Gentiles? As indeed he says in Hosea, 'Those who were not my people I will call "my people"… they shall be called children of the living God.'

As Paul looks at Israel's history, he sees a process of narrowing down. Some figures, such as Esau and Pharaoh (vv. 13, 17), were like rough splinters, pushed to one side by the chisel of God's purpose. Further, the nation itself was chiselled and planed thin over the centuries. It was a painful process, showing two sides to God's nature—wrath and mercy.

It was as if God wanted history to make two things plain: he takes sin seriously and means to deal with it; and he rejoices to embrace his people in mercy. Those two purposes eventually meet at the cross of Christ. In the Old Testament period, they seem to run side by side, as a persistent witness to the justice and the love of God.

Make no mistake, however, says Paul, about the larger and more decisive of these two themes. Love is the destination. God has 'endured with patience' the times when he had to judge, but all along he was preparing to 'make known his glory'. Finally, mercy will sound as the loudest and longest note in heaven, but, before then, mercy will gather Gentiles as well as Jews into the Church on earth. The story that began with Abraham ends with blessing reaching out across the earth (Genesis 12:3). Gentiles, who seemed to be outside the scope of grace, are gathered into the centre.

One of the joys of our day is the richness of the Church's international life. Contact, mail and transport reach swiftly around the earth, and many a local congregation reflects God's wide world in its membership . Paul would have revelled in this, as a marvellous sign of mercy and love.

### Reflection and prayer

*Thank God and pray for any Christians you know in other lands.*

JP

# Targets and tangles

What then are we to say? Gentiles, who did not strive for righteousness, have attained it, that is, righteousness through faith; but Israel, who did strive for the righteousness that is based on the law, did not succeed in fulfilling that law. Why not? Because they did not strive for it on the basis of faith, but as if it were based on works.

Through most of Romans 9, Paul has traced the purpose of God and all that he was doing across the centuries. Now Paul's line of thought moves on to explore a new angle. He starts to ask about people and the different ways in which they have responded to God. How is it, he wonders, that Gentiles have been gathered into the fold of faith, but the majority of Jewish people do not yet believe in Jesus?

A key word is 'righteousness'. Gentiles found it almost by accident, says Paul, while Israel aimed for it and missed. By 'righteousness' Paul means, first and foremost, a right relationship, a position of security and peace with God. Certainly such a relationship influences the way that we live, but it is not chiefly something we do for God; it is something God does for us. That is Paul's point.

Israel had a law and many of her people were serious about following it, but too many saw it as a matter of 'works'. The Law reached deep into daily life. It marked Jewish people out from their neighbours, particularly in terms of their intricate food laws and religious calendar of sabbaths and festivals. Paul sensed that those 'works'—what people tried to do for God—had attracted too much attention. For some, the Law had become a focus of concern in itself, rather than a way of nurturing trust and looking forward to the gospel.

Does all this feel far away from your situation and mine? Yes and no, for we have various customs and moral commitments as Christians and it is right that we do. Is there ever a danger, however, that they become our 'Law' and block our vision of God? If there is, might we, too, find ourselves pursuing a kind of 'works' and missing the main target of our faith?

### Prayer

*Lord, help us to keep our eyes fixed on Jesus, on whom our faith depends from start to finish (Hebrews 12:2).*

JP

# Faith value

If you confess with your lips that Jesus is Lord and believe in your heart that God raised him from the dead, you will be saved. For one believes with the heart and so is justified, and one confesses with the mouth and so is saved. The scripture says, 'No one who believes in him will be put to shame.' For there is no distinction between Jew and Greek; the same Lord is Lord of all and is generous to all who call on him. For, 'Everyone who calls on the name of the Lord shall be saved.'

In yesterday's reading, Paul wrote very positively about faith. Faith is the key to a right relationship with God. Faith is also the true meaning of the Law, the destination to which it was meant to lead. In today's verses we discover what Paul means by faith.

Many churches today use a creed in their services—a statement of the main points of Christian belief. Today's passage may well contain two brief statements of faith that were used by the earliest Christians. Here they are—two different ways of saying more or less the same thing.

'Jesus is Lord.' Faith looks to Jesus and rejoices in his person and power. He is Lord, sharing the dignity and glory of his Father, drawing the worship of heaven, claiming the love and praise of the Church. If this was an early creed, there is a trace of its use at 1 Corinthians 12:3, as well as here.

'God raised him from the dead.' This expression, or words very like it, crop up often in the New Testament (for example, Galatians 1:1). The earliest Christians were resurrection people; Easter was the centre of their faith. They spoke of Jesus as a living Lord because they believed he was risen.

For Paul, faith in the risen Jesus was vital. It was what gave the Church confidence and held it together. Jewish and Gentile Christians alike could share that belief. They would find that it bound them securely and firmly to Israel's God and to one another. Still, we are Easter people. To call Jesus Lord binds us in fellowship and brings us into the safety of God's love.

### Prayer

*Living Lord Jesus Christ, we thank you that your love and power are stronger than death.*

JP

# Footwork for God

But how are they to call on one in whom they have not believed? And how are they to believe in one of whom they have never heard? And how are they to hear without someone to proclaim him? And how are they to proclaim him unless they are sent? As it is written, 'How beautiful are the feet of those who bring good news!' But not all have obeyed the good news; for Isaiah says, 'Lord, who has believed our message?' So faith comes from what is heard, and what is heard comes through the word of Christ.

Yesterday's reading ended with a verse from the prophet Joel: 'Everyone who calls on the name of the Lord shall be saved.' By 'the Lord', Joel meant Israel's God. Then, when Paul took his text, he used it to speak of Jesus. The New Testament uses the Old in this way quite often. The risen Lord Jesus is one with God, in rule and love and life. To call on Jesus is, indeed, to call on God.

So, how will people call on Jesus? According to Paul, it usually comes as the last in a chain of events. Messengers are sent; they preach the word of Christ; people hear and believe; only then will they confess his name and discover his saving power. Of course, it can happen more directly. Paul's own conversion shows that (Acts 9), but most people come to faith because someone tells them about Jesus Christ and they take the time to listen.

That means messengers have a vital role. In every generation, the Church needs people with the gift and motivation to share the faith with others. We need those who will cross the sea to do this and others who do it over the garden fence or across a coffee table. Paul quotes two Old Testament texts to describe this work.

Sharing Christ's message is a beautiful task. You are a messenger of hope and gladness. Some hearers will thank you for bringing them good news and thank God that they met you. It is also a frustrating task, however, as success comes in patches, as it did for Jesus (Mark 4:3–9).

### Reflection and prayer

*Thank God for the people who taught you the faith. Pray for people who have heard the gospel from you.*

JP

# Stumbling blocks and stepping stones

So I ask, have they stumbled so as to fall? By no means! But through their stumbling salvation has come to the Gentiles, so as to make Israel jealous. Now if their stumbling means riches for the world, and if their defeat means riches for the Gentiles, how much more will their full inclusion mean! Now I am speaking to you Gentiles. Inasmuch then as I am an apostle to the Gentiles, I glorify my ministry in order to make my own people jealous, and thus save some of them.

In Romans 9, Paul looked back, to trace God's work in the past. In chapter 10, he looked around, at the spread of the good news in his own day. Now he looks forward. How will the life of the Church develop? What will become of God's commitment to Israel? Paul grieves that many of his fellow Israelites have not welcomed the message of Jesus. They have stumbled, he says, but that does not mean that the nation has lost its place in God's heart. They have not stumbled 'so as to fall'. There is a curious to and fro in God's purpose.

By a strange movement of grace, Israel's 'stumbling' has led to the sharing of the gospel among the Gentiles. We see some of this story in Acts (8:1–4; 11:19–26). As opposition in Jerusalem increased, Christians moved out and spread the faith as they went. A wide Gentile mission started and, by the time Paul wrote Romans (about AD57), there were little Christian communities in many towns of the Greek and Roman world.

Paul was heavily involved in this growing network of churches and here he writes about making the Jewish people 'jealous'. If they understand what God is doing among the Gentiles, he says, they will turn to Christ, which will complete the circle. Israel's 'stumbling', then, was a stage in the gospel reaching the world. The world's belief will help the good news find its way back to Israel.

All this reminds us what a complex and diverse world the gospel arrived in. The New Testament tells a rapid story of mission and cross-cultural outreach. God was reaching the earth with good news. In our day, the same God is still at work.

**Prayer**

*Pray that the life of your church helps others to know Christ.*

JP

# Branching in

But if some of the branches were broken off, and you, a wild olive shoot, were grafted in their place to share the rich root of the olive tree, do not vaunt yourselves over the branches. If you do vaunt yourselves, remember that it is not you that support the root, but the root that supports you… And even those of Israel, if they do not persist in unbelief, will be grafted in, for God has the power to graft them in again.

This trick of grafting a piece of wild olive on to a cultivated tree was sometimes tried by farmers at that time. If it worked, it could give the tree new energy and strength. Paul was using the picture of the olive as a symbol for Israel. He wanted his readers to think about where their faith had come from. The grafted branches were Gentile Christians.

Did some of the Gentile Christians in Rome reckon that they were better than some Jewish people because they believed in Jesus and the Jews did not? Did they think that, perhaps, God had moved on from Israel to concentrate on other nations? Did they 'vaunt… over the branches' that they thought had been broken off and discarded from God's olive tree? 'Don't think like that,' says Paul. 'Remember your spiritual roots.'

The Christian Church comes out of the Old Testament. Through its long story of grace, our faith began and the word took flesh. Jesus was Jewish and so were most of the people who wrote the Bible. It is right for us to honour that heritage. Sadly, however, the Church has not always treated Jewish people with respect and care. Most Christians today are not Jewish and, in some places, deep prejudices and painful memories still divide Jews and Christians.

Paul's vision invites us to recall where we come from, spiritually. He would surely urge us to pray for more Jewish people to believe in Jesus. He would certainly expect us, as Christians, to treat those Jewish people we know with respect and goodwill. Perhaps, too, he would remind us of the needs and sensitivities of Jewish Christians, whose concerns have not always been well understood by a mainly Gentile Church.

### Prayer

*Thank you, God, for Jesus, the light of the world, and for the people of Israel, among whom he was born.*

JP

# Two-way commitment

I appeal to you therefore, brothers and sisters, by the mercies of God, to present your bodies as a living sacrifice, holy and acceptable to God, which is your spiritual worship. Do not be conformed to this world, but be transformed by the renewing of your minds, so that you may discern what is the will of God—what is good and acceptable and perfect.

Here we move into a new section of the letter. Paul has laboured, right through chapters 9 to 11, to explain God's dealings with Israel. The final note is mercy (11:31–32). God's greatest work, the fullest expression of his character, is compassion, care and love. At the cross of Christ we see, and in time we shall discover, the immense and immeasurable mercies of God.

A God like this deserves the loving service of our lives. Paul urges his readers to commit themselves to God and live out God's will from day to day. That, he says, is like offering a sacrifice, a complete commitment to God, just as offering an animal sacrifice was in Old Testament worship. The difference is that Christians are called to be 'a living sacrifice'. We give ourselves to God through the active commitment of our lives. That is 'spiritual worship', a dedication of will and heart.

Worship of this kind will change your mind, says Paul. We need not have our attitudes moulded by the world around, the fashions and feelings of other people, but we can be gradually and genuinely changed. We can learn to look at the world through God's eyes and think about life with the mind of Christ. Then we shall recognize God's will more truly and surely and tackle the duties and decisions of each day in ways that please and serve God.

The next few chapters of this letter are very practical, concerned with everyday issues such as lifestyle, neighbours, money and quarrels, but dealing with practical matters is a spiritual issue, too. It starts with commitment, to the God who committed himself to us in the cross of Christ.

### Prayer

*Lord of all wisdom, help me to see with your eyes the people I meet. Help me to touch with your goodness the places I go. Help me to discover your will as I live in your world.*

JP

ROMANS 12:4–10 (NRSV)

# Body beautiful

For as in one body we have many members, and not all the members have the same function, so we, who are many, are one body in Christ, and individually we are members one of another. We have gifts that differ according to the grace given to us: prophecy, in proportion to faith; ministry, in ministering; the teacher, in teaching; the exhorter, in exhortation; the giver, in generosity; the leader, in diligence; the compassionate, in cheerfulness. Let love be genuine; hate what is evil, hold fast to what is good; love one another with mutual affection; outdo one another in showing honour.

Christian commitment needs to be personal—yesterday's reading showed that—but it is not private. Commitment to Jesus brings us into a community of believers. The Church is one body in Christ and that is both a privilege and a responsibility. My living is bound up with the lives of other Christians. We depend on each other.

I wonder if Paul's idea of the Church as the body of Christ, which appears several times in his letters, goes back to his conversion. He heard a voice saying, 'Saul, Saul, why do you persecute me?' (Acts 9:4). From then on he started to realize that the Church belonged to Jesus. In its life was the life of the risen Christ.

According to our reading today, there are two things that we can do to keep the body healthy. One is to contribute to its life with our gifts and service. Today's verses list a number of gifts that help to sustain the Church: encouragement, teaching, leading, sharing, caring. Each person has something to give to the life of the body and each person can receive from the involvement of others.

The other thing that sustains the Church is love. Gifts without love would count for nothing (1 Corinthians 13:2). We are called to a genuine and generous Christian love, a practical care of heart and hand for one another. Love is not careless. It takes good and evil seriously and makes a steady effort to avoid wrong and embrace what is right. It also values other people and aims to respect and enjoy what each one brings to the life of the body.

**Prayer**

*Thank God for the people in your local church who bring this text to life for you.*

JP

# Peace of the Lord

Bless those who persecute you; bless and do not curse them. Rejoice with those who rejoice, weep with those who weep. Live in harmony with one another; do not be haughty, but associate with the lowly; do not claim to be wiser than you are. Do not repay anyone evil for evil, but take thought for what is noble in the sight of all. If it is possible, so far as it depends on you, live peaceably with all.

Quotations from the teachings of Jesus are quite rare in Paul. There are strong connections between Jesus' message and Paul's thinking, but not many direct quotes. Yet, in these last chapters of Romans, quite a number of phrases seem to echo Jesus' own words. 'Pray for those who persecute you,' said Jesus (Matthew 5:44). 'Do not resist an evildoer. But if anyone strikes you on the right cheek, turn the other also' (v. 39). This very practical teaching had been remembered and handed down. Paul uses it here to remind the Church about the Christian lifestyle. Christians' attitudes, outlook and dealings with others should reflect the Lord they serve.

The standard is high. A Christian tries to avoid being nasty to others, even when they seem to deserve it. A Christian aims to enter positively into the moods and needs of other people, sharing as far as possible their joys and sorrows. A Christian seeks to live at peace with other people and steer clear of quarrels and ill feeling. A Christian is not a snob—never too proud to enjoy a neighbour's company, never so sure of his or her own wisdom as to ignore everyone else.

All that must have been particularly hard for some of Paul's readers in Rome. They had been caught up in some serious public disorder a few years before and there would be a terrible spell of violent persecution not many years ahead. There must have been a steady undercurrent of opposition and unpleasantness throughout this period. The only way to handle it, says Paul, is with goodwill and good deeds. Two thousand years later, there are still Christians who are under that sort of pressure, some of them more or less constantly. They deserve our prayers and, if we can, our help.

### Prayer

*Pray for Christians you know, or know of, who face opposition and anger for their faith. Ask that they be faithful under fire.*

JP

# Power with a purpose

Let every person be subject to the governing authorities; for there is no authority except from God, and those authorities that exist have been instituted by God. Therefore whoever resists authority resists what God has appointed, and those who resist will incur judgment. For rulers are not a terror to good conduct, but to bad. Do you wish to have no fear of the authority? Then do what is good, and you will receive its approval; for it is God's servant for your good... Pay to all what is due to them—taxes to whom taxes are due, revenue to whom revenue is due, respect to whom respect is due, honour to whom honour is due.

Taxes were rising in Rome and nobody liked it. Around the time of this letter, there was unrest over demands made by the government and its agents. Eventually the emperor had to lower the rates, to ease the burden on the people. Paul seems to have heard about this agitation and warned the Christians not to get drawn in. The Church was a fragile movement at that time and much damage could be done if they attracted the wrong kind of attention. However awkward the government was, Christians would gain little from undertaking any kind of organized resistance.

Paul himself had a series of scrapes with various civic authorities (Acts 16—19). He realized that public reactions to the Christian message were unpredictable. It was important not to cause unnecessary offence over an issue not directly connected to the gospel, so here he reminds us of two reasons for obeying the State. One is fear: the State has power and should be treated with respect. The other is faith: the State has a purpose and should be given support in fulfilling it.

Government, according to these verses, is a gift of God. It is there for the sake of order, goodness and justice. Rulers have a task and they need help to do it properly. Certainly the Bible also speaks critically about governments; at times criticism is fair. For most of us, most of the time, however, we serve God rightly by paying our taxes, keeping the law and praying for those in charge.

### Prayer

*Pray 'for all who are in high positions, so that we may lead a quiet and peaceable life in all godliness and dignity' (1 Timothy 2:2).*

JP

# Law of love

> Owe no one anything, except to love one another; for the one who loves another has fulfilled the law. The commandments, 'You shall not commit adultery; You shall not murder; You shall not steal; You shall not covet'; and any other commandment, are summed up in this word, 'Love your neighbour as yourself.' Love does no wrong to a neighbour; therefore, love is the fulfilling of the law.

Love is a major theme throughout Romans. God has given us his love, in the death of Jesus Christ and through the coming of the Holy Spirit (5:5, 8). Christians love God and we know that the love God gave us in Jesus cannot be taken away (8:28, 35, 39). Love is a two-way bond, linking our lives to God's.

Love is also a gift to pass on, a thing of warmth and energy. 'Let love be genuine,' said Paul (12:9). The verses that follow talk of how to do this: by Christian care (vv. 10–13), in times of opposition and difficulty (vv. 14–21) and as tax-payers and citizens (13:1–7). Genuine love binds Christians one to another and strengthens the Church's life. It reaches out to neighbours and responds graciously, even in the face of criticism. Today's reading talks of love as a gift of the past and a task for the present.

'Love is the fulfilling of the law'—Israel's ancient Law. Paul quotes four of the Ten Commandments (from Exodus 20), and then explains that all the Law's commands are summed up in one: 'Love your neighbour as yourself.' That sort of summary of the Law appears elsewhere—in Matthew 22:34–40, for example, and in some Jewish teachings of that time. Paul tells it that way to remind his readers that love is a value they have in common. Whatever their backgrounds, whether they are Jewish or Gentile, they need not be divided by law, but can be united by love.

'Owe no one anything, except… love.' Even when yesterday's work is done and today's taxes have been paid, there will still be tomorrow's love to give. Every new day we owe this to Christ and our neighbour. Love is always a duty and often a delight. We give the love we have received from God, through Jesus Christ.

### Prayer

*God of love, help me to love the people I meet today.*

JP

# Light duty

Besides this, you know what time it is, how it is now the moment for you to wake from sleep. For salvation is nearer to us now than when we became believers; the night is far gone, the day is near. Let us then lay aside the works of darkness and put on the armour of light; let us live honourably as in the day, not in revelling and drunkenness, not in debauchery and licentiousness, not in quarrelling and jealousy. Instead, put on the Lord Jesus Christ, and make no provision for the flesh, to gratify its desires.

Part of our previous reading spoke of Christian love from the perspective of the past. Love, it said, fulfils Israel's Law (v. 10). What God gave then finds its full meaning now. Love brings tradition to life and puts one of God's oldest gifts into lively practice.

The verses here point to the future. What God will do tomorrow can motivate us today. The world is travelling towards the light. God's day is coming, a day of glory and judgment when the world will know Jesus as Lord and creation will rejoice. 'Hope' is what Paul calls it elsewhere in Romans (5:5; 8:18–25), and hope has power. It gives energy and a sense of purpose when we believe that time is in God's hands.

Paul writes of night and day as two ways of living. 'Night life' for him is not about what we do after sunset. It means living without the light of God, as if God never sees us and has done nothing to guide

us into right ways. 'Night life' is wasting what God has given us and carping at God's goodness to other people. That is a way of life that we should 'put off', as surely as we change what we wear when we get up in the morning.

'Day clothes' for the Christian, the life we are to put on, is the pattern of living outlined in Romans 12 and 13. If we live like that, we are ready for the day ahead. Of course, we cannot do it ourselves. It is Christ's life and love, flowing through us. That is why it says, 'Put on the Lord Jesus Christ.'

### Reflection and prayer

*'You know what time it is.' Think over, with God, if it is time to make changes to the way you live.*

JP

# Answering to God

Welcome those who are weak in faith, but not for the purpose of quarrelling over opinions. Some believe in eating anything, while the weak eat only vegetables. Those who eat must not despise those who abstain, and those who abstain must not pass judgment on those who eat; for God has welcomed them. Who are you to pass judgment on servants of another? It is before their own Lord that they stand or fall. And they will be upheld, for the Lord is able to make them stand.

Towards the end of the letter, we find some very direct pastoral advice for the Christians in Rome. Theirs was a divided fellowship and Paul wanted to draw them together. Chapter 11 speaks of a tree with a new branch—Jewish and Gentile Christians grafted into one in Christ. Chapters 12 and 13 stress the importance of love. Here in chapter 14, Paul says, 'Welcome one another. Show your love in practice. Live as one spiritual family, even though you have different opinions on some issues.'

By 'welcome', Paul probably meant that Christians should receive one another into their homes. The Church met in members' houses, so it was important that they should be able to gather without restriction. Hospitality— the open door, open heart and open table—should not depend on a person's ethnic or cultural background.

Some were 'weak in faith'—I think by this Paul meant Christians with a strong Jewish background, who had known the Law all their lives and would not break with their ancestral tradition. If they dined with Gentiles, they would 'eat only vegetables' as they could not be sure that the meat was kosher. Perhaps, as well, some Gentile Christians called them 'weak' and did not understand their hesitations.

Paul tells each side to respect the other. If God has accepted them, then they cannot do otherwise. We answer to God, Paul says, and we should allow our fellow Christians to do the same. Indeed, accepting one another, without seeking to argue or dispute, is part of answering to God. It responds to God's love in Christ and our Christian fellowship reflects the gospel.

### Reflection and prayer

*Can you hold out the hand of Christian friendship to someone whose views differ from yours?*

JP

# Taking care, giving care

I know and am persuaded in the Lord Jesus that nothing is unclean in itself; but it is unclean for anyone who thinks it unclean. If your brother or sister is being injured by what you eat, you are no longer walking in love. Do not let what you eat cause the ruin of one for whom Christ died. So do not let your good be spoken of as evil. For the kingdom of God is not food and drink but righteousness and peace and joy in the Holy Spirit.

The whole of Romans 14 is about Christian fellowship—about honouring one another, even when opinions and background differ—but there is a change of focus as the chapter goes on. Yesterday's verses put the emphasis on neighbours: how do I regard a Christian who behaves differently from me? If one eats and another abstains, says Paul, they should still accept each other. Today's reading, however, is about your own lifestyle: how do you appear in other people's eyes? Does any habit of yours cause trouble for Christians around you?

It seems that some Gentile Christians in Rome had a very confident approach to meat eating: 'Never mind how it's been slaughtered. So what if part of the carcase was sacrificed in a pagan temple? It's God's creation, so it's clean. Now, will you have one slice or two?' That attitude was likely to really upset Jewish Christians. It would feel like a betrayal of their tradition and some might want to leave that Christian fellowship over the issue.

So, Paul urges caution. Watch how you live. Acceptance is not just putting up with someone else's ways. It means making sure that you do not lead anyone astray by doing something that seems harmless and normal to you. 'Meat is clean,' says Paul, 'but even things God created need to be used with care.' Taking care can be a way to give care.

Meat may not be an issue for you or your local church, but care certainly should be. You should think, 'Is there anything I do, anywhere I go, any company I keep, that makes it harder for a sister or brother to hold the faith?'

Our verses today seem to be about food, but really they are about fellowship.

### Prayer
*Pray for anyone you know who is struggling to stay on the Christian road.*

JP

# One people of praise

Welcome one another, therefore, just as Christ has welcomed you, for the glory of God. For I tell you that Christ has become a servant of the circumcised on behalf of the truth of God in order that he might confirm the promises given to the patriarchs, and in order that the Gentiles might glorify God for his mercy. As it is written, '… The root of Jesse shall come, the one who rises to rule the Gentiles; in him the Gentiles shall hope.'

Our last two readings were about Christian belonging. Two groups of believers were called to be one in Christ and reflect that in their living. Love, care and consideration were the themes of chapter 14. Now we see Paul summing up this section of the letter in a mood of joy and hope. 'Welcome one another,' he says, 'as Christ has welcomed you.' The good news of Jesus Christ gathers the story of scripture together. It forms one people of praise, from Israel and the nations, too.

Jesus came as 'servant of the circumcised'. The people of Israel could trace their line through almost 2000 years, back to their founding fathers, Abraham, Isaac and Jacob. God had promised that blessing would come to the world from their line, and now the promise was being realized. Jesus the Messiah had come and, through him, Israel's life would spread across the earth.

The text Paul quotes in verse 12, about 'the root of Jesse', is from the prophet Isaiah. Jesse had been King David's father, so Paul's point in using that text is to name Jesus as a new David, a royal leader in Israel, a king among his people. Yet Jesus came not to them alone, but for all the peoples on earth. By activating God's ancient promise to Israel, he gives hope to Jew and Gentile alike and brings them together as one choir of praise, rejoicing in heaven's mercy.

These verses are full of confidence and gladness. God keeps his word. History has a centre and a purpose. The nations are gathered. There is hope. We surely have much to celebrate when we welcome one another in the name of Jesus Christ.

**Prayer**

*Lord, may your Church rejoice
in the promises you have kept
in the past and the hope you offer
for the future.*

JP

# Journey man

For I will not venture to speak of anything except what Christ has accomplished through me to win obedience from the Gentiles, by word and deed, by the power of signs and wonders, by the power of the Spirit of God, so that from Jerusalem and as far around as Illyricum I have fully proclaimed the good news of Christ... This is the reason that I have so often been hindered from coming to you. But now, with no further place for me in these regions, I desire, as I have for many years, to come to you when I go to Spain.

Paul rounds off this letter, as we sometimes do ourselves, with personal news. He picks up a thread he laid down at the very start of Romans (1:8–15) and talks about his plans to visit Rome and meet the Christians there. That would be new ground for him; he had never been to Rome before, although he had often wanted to go there.

Paul was already widely travelled. Jerusalem is a name we know—the pilgrim capital of Israel. Illyricum, which covers the lands we call Bosnia and Croatia, is roughly a thousand miles from Jerusalem and Paul did much of that distance on foot. He never lost the desire to spread the Christian gospel, especially to places it had never reached before.

Paul's forthcoming journey to Spain would be another thousand miles or so further west and, indeed, the roundabout sea route he planned would take him much further than that (see tomorrow's reading). There would be a chance, though, to pause in Rome, encourage the Christians there and secure their help for the next stage of his work.

Paul aimed to make the gospel known by 'word and deed': he would speak of God's power and show that power at work. By 'signs and wonders' he probably meant acts of healing. As he went about, Paul expected the Holy Spirit to work through him. Even though much has changed in church life since then, some things remain constant: the call to proclaim Christ in word and action and our need to trust and rely on the Spirit of God.

**Prayer**

*Holy Spirit of God, will you give the Church power and courage in our day, to make Jesus Christ known by word and deed.*

JP

# Cheerful givers

For I do hope to see you on my journey and to be sent on by you, once I have enjoyed your company for a little while. At present, however, I am going to Jerusalem in a ministry to the saints; for Macedonia and Achaia have been pleased to share their resources with the poor among the saints at Jerusalem. They were pleased to do this, and indeed they owe it to them; for if the Gentiles have come to share in their spiritual blessings, they ought also to be of service to them in material things.

Paul was probably writing from Greece, from the town of Corinth, so, when he wrote about going to Rome, that would require a journey westwards. First, however, he intended to head east, to Jerusalem. That voyage would be part of a major project, which Paul mentions several times in his letters, and it was clearly an important element in his life's work. The project involved collection of money.

There had been food shortages in the holy land and Christians there were in serious need. So, as Paul founded and nurtured churches elsewhere, he asked those believers to contribute to the needs of their spiritual brothers and sisters in Israel. Many did so. Paul mentions Macedonia and Achaia— roughly speaking, northern and southern Greece—but it appears that others gave, too, as, when he set sail, he was accompanied by friends from several different churches, over a wide area (Acts 20:4). Companions would help with security, but they would also represent the givers when the gift was handed over.

Paul thought of that gift as a sign of belonging. Christians from different backgrounds, in the Gentile world and in Israel, would be linked by their act of kindness. It was, in a way, the repayment of a debt. The gospel had come from Israel to the Gentiles and the gift was one way to say thank you.

'Saints' is what Paul calls the church in Jerusalem. The word means 'holy people', but Paul does not mean Christians of unusual gifts or importance. He means that any and every Christian is made holy by belonging to Jesus.

### Reflection

*Think about signs of care, appreciation and respect that people have shown you. Then, consider what you could do to offer the same to others.*

JP

# Life savers

I commend to you our sister Phoebe, a deacon of the church at Cenchreae, so that you may welcome her in the Lord as is fitting for the saints, and help her in whatever she may require from you, for she has been a benefactor of many and of myself as well. Greet Prisca and Aquila, who work with me in Christ Jesus, and who risked their necks for my life, to whom not only I give thanks, but also all the churches of the Gentiles.

This last chapter has many personal greetings. As Paul mentions these people, his words often give a little portrait of each person's character. Phoebe was surely a warm and generous person. She belonged to Cenchreae, a port near Corinth, and was probably the one who carried this letter to Rome. In Cenchreae she was a 'deacon of the church', trusted by her fellow Christians in a role of responsibility and care. She was also a 'benefactor' of many.

This word 'benefactor' means a person who notices and assists with the concerns of others. It suggests that Phoebe had wealth and was ready to use it when friends were in need. She had helped Paul, too. He often worked to support himself in his missionary work, but he welcomed gifts from people he felt he could trust. Phoebe seems to have been a woman of substance, integrity and kindness.

Prisca (also called Priscilla) and Aquila pop up in several places in the New Testament. They worked with Paul in Corinth and helped Apollos, a gifted but erratic preacher, to get himself straight (Acts 18). Wherever they went, their home became a meeting place for Christians. They must have been friendly and sensible—welcoming, willing to listen, prepared to deal with trouble—and their care had real depth. We know nothing about the occasion when they 'risked their necks' for Paul's sake, but he remembered it. Courage and love of that kind always leave a mark.

Happy is the church that has people like Phoebe, Prisca and Aquila in its ranks. Their influences created confidence, trust and strength around the whole fellowship. They may not have stood out in a crowd, but their attitude and service were special indeed.

### Prayer

*Thank God for the people in your church who are generous with money, friendship and care.*

JP

# Glory and gratitude

Now to God who is able to strengthen you according to my gospel and the proclamation of Jesus Christ, according to the revelation of the mystery that was kept secret for long ages but is now disclosed, and through the prophetic writings is made known to all the Gentiles, according to the command of the eternal God, to bring about the obedience of faith—to the only wise God, through Jesus Christ, to whom be the glory for ever! Amen.

The greetings are over. Thirty-five names have been mentioned in this chapter, as Paul reminds the church of the many personal links and contacts he shares with them. Even though he has not been to Rome, he will not come as an unknown figure. His letter and forthcoming visit are expressions of deep and informed pastoral care.

Now, as Paul signs off, he looks upwards and gives praise to God. He is grateful for the good news of Jesus Christ and the immense privilege of sharing it across the world. Out of its hiding place in the purposes of God, the gospel has been brought into the open through the coming of Jesus. Out of the pages of Israel's ancient scriptures, the message has stretched out to the nations. As a word that calls people to faith, the good news leads believers on into obedience and active goodness. As Paul gives praise to the eternal God, he rejoices that this God is near, to strengthen the people in Rome for whom he cares.

God can hold these Christians together, as a welcoming people, as Jew and Gentile joined in one body. God can give them courage and calm, to live in love, even when neighbours do not welcome their faith. God can keep them as a people of hope, sure and secure until the morning comes (13:12).

The final chapters of Romans have brought us some very practical messages. They have reminded us that Christians belong together —although we are a very diverse company, from different backgrounds, we are one body in Christ. They have challenged us to live as a people of love. They have ended with a note of confidence, faith and praise to the God of the gospel of Jesus Christ.

**Prayer**

*To the only wise God, through Jesus Christ, be the glory for ever!*

JP

# Sin and salvation

A taciturn man went to church while his wife cooked the Sunday roast. When he got home, his wife asked what the sermon had been about. 'Sin,' grunted her husband. 'And what did he have to say about it?' she enquired. 'He were agin it,' came the reply.

Well, I would hope we're all 'agin' sin and for salvation. So, what more is there to say? Plenty, in a world where the word 'sin' is rarely used and where 'salvation' can be reduced to no more than how we answer the question 'Are you saved?' In fact, as I discovered in writing these notes, a week is not really enough to do justice to either of these themes. Viewed from one angle, the whole Bible is about sin and, from another, the whole of it is about salvation.

Where does sin come from? What makes us so prone to doing wrong? Is sin just about what we do or is it also about what and how we think and feel? What does it mean to say that we are all sinners? Is salvation mainly about the forgiveness of sins or is there more? Are we mainly saved 'from' something or are we also saved 'for' something?

I certainly haven't provided exhaustive answers to these big questions—even a whole theological library couldn't do that. Instead, I have picked well-known and less familiar scripture passages to provide some preliminary pointers to answers—or, indeed, raise some questions that are not often asked.

Perhaps it's good that I was only given a week's readings for each subject. Too much talk about sin can load us down with guilt and make us forget that we are forgiven. Perhaps, however, there can never be too much talk about salvation, although stressing our salvation without also recognizing that we are far from fully sanctified could make us complacent.

So, I have tried to create a balance between acknowledging our own failures and rejoicing that we are accepted as God's children, and between knowing that we are safe in God's hands and confessing that we, and the world, have a long way to go before we experience the true fullness of salvation. For just as sin is a pandemic that has infected the whole world, so salvation is God's project for healing—not just a minority of individuals, but the whole world, starting with us.

*Veronica Zundel*

GENESIS 2:16–17; 3:6–8 (NRSV)

# Knowing too much

The Lord God commanded the man, 'You may freely eat of every tree of the garden; but of the tree of the knowledge of good and evil you shall not eat...' ... When the woman saw that the tree was good for food, and that it was a delight to the eyes, and that the tree was to be desired to make one wise, she took of its fruit and ate; and she also gave some to her husband, who was with her, and he ate. Then the eyes of both were opened, and they knew that they were naked; and they sewed fig leaves together and made loincloths for themselves. They heard the sound of the Lord God walking in the garden at the time of the evening breeze, and the man and his wife hid themselves from the presence of the Lord God among the trees of the garden.

All of us who are parents want our children to know right and wrong—why would God not want his first children to know the same?

Here's how I look at it: Adam and Eve already know good, in the goodness of the world God has created (Genesis 1:31). In the words of 17th-century writer Thomas Traherne, they know 'no churlish properties, nor bounds, nor divisions'. Their view of the world is as pure as that of a newborn child. Knowing evil makes them recognizably human—divided beings just like we are—yet it is a great loss that leads to them hiding from each other and God, then each blaming the other for their disobedience.

What does this say about our understanding of sin? Perhaps sin is about taking instead of receiving; grabbing for ourselves something God has not given us yet, because we are not ready for it. The knowledge of good and evil has been a very mixed experience for humankind. Too often we have labelled others as evil and rejected, even exterminated, them.

### Reflection

*'Certainly Adam in Paradise had not more sweet and curious apprehensions of the world, than I when I was a child... So that with much ado I was corrupted, and made to learn the dirty devices of this world. Which now I unlearn, and become, as it were, a little child again that I may enter into the Kingdom of God'*

Thomas Traherne, *Centuries*

VZ

GENESIS 3:14–18 (NRSV)

# How we live now

The Lord God said to the serpent, 'Because you have done this, cursed are you among all animals... upon your belly you shall go, and dust you shall eat all the days of your life. I will put enmity between you and the woman, and between your offspring and hers; he will strike your head, and you will strike his heel.' To the woman he said, 'I will greatly increase your pangs in childbearing... yet your desire shall be for your husband, and he shall rule over you.' And to the man he said, 'Because you have listened to the voice of your wife, and have eaten of the tree about which I commanded you, "You shall not eat of it", cursed is the ground because of you; in toil you shall eat of it all the days of your life; thorns and thistles it shall bring forth for you; and you shall eat the plants of the field.'

I was only five when my parents bought the land for their 'dream house', but I remember the hours they spent hacking back brambles to uncover what had once been a garden and orchard. 'Thorns and thistles' indeed!

Contrary to popular assumption, Adam and Eve are not cursed after the Fall; only the serpent and the ground are cursed. To the human beings, God simply predicts how things will be from now on.

The whole thing reads like one of Rudyard Kipling's 'Just So' stories about how various animals acquired their strange characteristics. It is not a child's fable, though, but a horror story. Pace Douglas Adams, our planet is not 'mostly harmless', but a place where nature is, in Tennyson's words, 'red in tooth and claw'; where humans and environment are estranged, childbearing is painful and risky and work is often sheer back-breaking slog. Most of the world still has no modern medicine or machinery.

It is a story of how sin damages our best human abilities and efforts. Whether we believe that Adam and Eve were actual historical beings or not, we can recognize it as a profoundly accurate portrayal of the world we live in—and to know that, to a great extent, we have made it that way.

### Prayer

*'We have sinned against you and against our neighbours, in thought and word and deed.'*

Anglican Confession

VZ

# Offerings

In the course of time Cain brought to the Lord an offering of the fruit of the ground, and Abel for his part brought of the firstlings of his flock... And the Lord had regard for Abel and his offering, but for Cain and his offering he had no regard. So Cain was very angry, and his countenance fell. The Lord said to Cain, 'Why are you angry...? If you do well, will you not be accepted? And if you do not do well, sin is lurking at the door; its desire is for you, but you must master it.' Cain said to his brother Abel, 'Let us go out to the field.' And when they were in the field, Cain rose up against his brother Abel and killed him. Then the Lord said to Cain, 'Where is your brother Abel?' He said, 'I do not know; am I my brother's keeper?' And the Lord said, 'What have you done? Listen; your brother's blood is crying out to me from the ground!'

Here's another mysterious story. Why does God not accept Cain's offering? We can't know, but notice that God's address to Cain does not say that his offering is unacceptable. Rather, God questions Cain's attitude. He has fulfilled his 'religious duty' to give an offering, but in his heart there is resentment brewing against his brother. If he could let go of his anger, the implication is that his offering would become a true gift to God.

I see a forerunner here of the prophets' teaching: 'Even though you offer me your burnt offerings and grain offerings, I will not accept them... But let justice roll down like waters, and righteousness like an ever-flowing stream' (Amos 5:22–24). Also, Jesus, in the prophetic tradition, declares, 'Out of the heart come evil intentions, murder, adultery, fornication, theft, false witness, slander. These are what defile a person' (Matthew 15:19–20).

These words tell us that sin is not a matter of performing or failing to perform particular actions. Rather, it is a condition, made up of the attitudes and habitual thoughts that inhabit the core of our being and issue in our actions. Of course, our acts also influence our attitudes, as we grow accustomed to living in a particular way.

### Reflection

*Who is our brother or sister?*
*Are we their keeper?*

VZ

# Sex and violence in the Bible

Cain knew his wife, and she conceived and bore Enoch; and he built a city, and named it Enoch after his son Enoch. To Enoch was born Irad; and Irad was the father of Mehujael, and Mehujael the father of Methushael, and Methushael the father of Lamech. Lamech took two wives; the name of one was Adah, and the name of the other Zillah… Lamech said to his wives: 'Adah and Zillah, hear my voice; you wives of Lamech, listen to what I say: I have killed a man for wounding me, a young man for striking me. If Cain is avenged sevenfold, truly Lamech seventy-sevenfold.'

I wonder what would happen if the Bible were published today for the first time. I suspect that there would be a lot of 'moral' people wanting to ban this potent mix of religion, sex and violence!

Lamech's story is rarely preached on, yet it is a concentrated picture of how sin affects our relations with others. Lamech is the Bible's first practitioner of polygamy—a system in which women are collected like prize cattle to show one's wealth and power. Note that telling phrase, 'took two wives', which suggests a tendency to treat women as objects.

Lamech is also our earliest example of the tendency for violence to escalate. How far is it from Lamech's macho threat, apparently voiced to impress his wives, to our own threat of 'mutually assured destruction'? An eye for an eye, a tooth for a tooth (Leviticus 24:20) was devised to limit that kind of vendetta culture, so no more than a just punishment would be inflicted.

So, we see relations between men and women, and relations between neighbours, tainted with pride, domination, aggression and self-centredness. Sin is never harmless: even if the immediate effects don't seem to be much, every unloving act contributes to an unloving society and so creates new unloving acts.

Though it was Lamech's ancestor, the murderer Cain, who built the first city, the Bible's view of cities is not all negative. Indeed, cities in the Bible are places of safety and fruitful relations between people. The new Jerusalem (Revelation 21) is a city where domination and violence have been destroyed and peace reigns.

### Prayer

*Lord, make our violent, lonely cities into places of peace and love.*

VZ

# God gives up?

The Lord saw that the wickedness of humankind was great in the earth, and that every inclination of the thoughts of their hearts was only evil continually. And the Lord was sorry that he had made humankind on the earth, and it grieved him to his heart. So the Lord said, 'I will blot out from the earth the human beings I have created—people together with animals and creeping things and birds of the air, for I am sorry that I have made them.' But Noah found favour in the sight of the Lord.

My son is a perfectionist. Often when he makes something—a drawing, perhaps—and a bit of it goes wrong, he angrily destroys the whole lot rather than trying to fix it.

Is that the kind of frustrated anger that God is displaying here? Is God merely being petulant and, in effect, saying, 'Oh bother the lot of them; they won't behave so I'll exterminate them'?

The story suggests otherwise: 'the Lord was sorry... it grieved him to his heart'. This is God as parent, lamenting that his children have gone so far astray. 'Every inclination... only evil... continually...'; does that mean, as some would say, that there is no good at all remaining in humankind, that we are incapable of ever acting in any way God counts as good? I don't think so; the language is typical Middle Eastern overstatement, stressing how pervasive the corruption of human beings is—so much so that even the natural world is damaged. 'All our righteous deeds are like a filthy cloth' (Isaiah 64:6) is a relative, not an absolute statement: compared to God, we are like dirty rags.

Yet, we are made in God's image and God finds one holy man to help him rescue the creation. This is the Bible's earliest salvation story, used by two New Testament writers as a picture of our redemption in Christ (Hebrews 11:7; 1 Peter 3:18–20). Sin is insidious, devious, but it is not the winner. God's love is greater than any evil we could devise.

### Reflection

*'For I do not do the good I want, but the evil I do not want is what I do... Wretched man that I am! Who will rescue me from this body of death? Thanks be to God through Jesus Christ our Lord!'*
*(Romans 7:19, 24–25).*

VZ

# Sin is personal

Have mercy on me, O God, according to your steadfast love; according to your abundant mercy blot out my transgressions. Wash me thoroughly from my iniquity, and cleanse me from my sin. For I know my transgressions, and my sin is ever before me. Against you, you alone, have I sinned, and done what is evil in your sight, so that you are justified in your sentence and blameless when you pass judgment. Indeed, I was born guilty, a sinner when my mother conceived me. You desire truth in the inward being; therefore teach me wisdom in my secret heart. Purge me with hyssop, and I shall be clean; wash me, and I shall be whiter than snow.

Wait a minute... isn't this psalm identified in its heading as what David wrote after he had committed adultery with Bathsheba and arranged for her husband to be killed in battle? Yet here he is, saying that he has sinned against God and God alone. What about Bathsheba (who seems to have had no choice in the matter) and her unfortunate husband, Uriah? Surely they, too, were victims of David's 'sex and power' game?

When we commit a sin—losing our temper with a family member or failing to stand up for justice in our workplace or telling less than the truth or manipulating someone to get our own way—we usually feel guiltiest about the person or people we have harmed. Yet, Jesus says that every time we fail to care for another, it is God we are abusing or neglecting (Matthew 25:31–46). Every sin against humans is, ulti-

mately, a sin against God.

Like Lady Macbeth washing her hands, David feels contaminated by his own actions and longs to be clean. His wrongdoing is constantly on his mind. He recognizes that he has been a sinner all his life (I don't personally think we should read this as a doctrinal statement of original sin passed on at conception, but just an acknowledgment that we all fall short). Yet, even as he wrestles with his guilt, he catches glimpses of God's mercy, which alone can change him.

Because we are weak and fallible, we will never, this side of the grave, give up sinning. Nevertheless, we still have choices and are responsible for our actions.

### Prayer
*'Lord, have mercy on me, a sinner'*
*(Luke 18:13).*

VZ

# Sin is social

Thus says the Lord: For three transgressions of Judah, and for four, I will not revoke the punishment; because they have rejected the law of the Lord, and have not kept his statutes, but they have been led astray by the same lies after which their ancestors walked. So I will send a fire on Judah, and it shall devour the strongholds of Jerusalem. Thus says the Lord: For three transgressions of Israel, and for four, I will not revoke the punishment; because they sell the righteous for silver, and the needy for a pair of sandals—they who trample the head of the poor into the dust of the earth, and push the afflicted out of the way; father and son go in to the same girl, so that my holy name is profaned; they lay themselves down beside every altar on garments taken in pledge; and in the house of their God they drink wine bought with fines they imposed.

Open any newspaper and you will see headlines about some leader or organization pronouncing judgment on some other country or group or warning of troubles to come: 'UN condemns genocide', 'Minister's speech blames unions', 'Environmentalists predict climate chaos'.

The opening of Amos' book of prophecy reads like a newspaper today. It is a continuous blast of judgment against the nations among whom the Jews lived: Syria, Gaza, Tyre, Edom, the Ammonites, Moab. Any Jews listening to it might have felt reassured that their enemies were to get their comeuppance.

Then Amos turns on Israel and Judah, God's own people, who are already divided by political and religious rivalry. These are the ones called to be 'a light to the nations' (Isaiah 49:5–6), yet they are guilty of unjust trade, contempt for the poor, sexual exploitation, abusing those in debt (a cloak taken in pledge was supposed to be returned at night as a blanket) and making unfair profit out of fines in court. Sound at all familiar?

Sin is always committed by individuals, but their actions contribute to oppressive systems and degraded cultures, and those systems and cultures lead others into sin. Both Old and New Testaments are very clear that the social and political dimensions of sin are as important as its personal consequences.

### Reflection

*What are the social and political sins of our country and world?*

VZ

42

# Saved from oppression

Then Moses stretched out his hand over the sea. The Lord drove the sea back by a strong east wind all night, and turned the sea into dry land; and the waters were divided. The Israelites went into the sea on dry ground... Then the Lord said to Moses, 'Stretch out your hand over the sea, so that the water may come back upon the Egyptians, upon their chariots and chariot drivers.' ... Then Moses and the Israelites sang this song to the Lord: 'I will sing to the Lord, for he has triumphed gloriously; horse and rider he has thrown into the sea. The Lord is my strength and my might, and he has become my salvation; this is my God, and I will praise him, my father's God, and I will exalt him. The Lord is a warrior; the Lord is his name.'

Every Eastertide, my church hosts two or three 'seders'—Passover meals in which we recall the great liberation of the Jews from exile in Egypt and draw parallels with our freedom in Christ and the last supper. A central part of the meal is the retelling of the exodus story, traditionally done by the father of the family.

The Old Testament's earliest understanding of salvation is being saved from enemies and the archetype of that salvation is the escape from Egypt and the crossing of the Red (or Reed) Sea. It was to be followed by many other victories in battle and, each time, the Israelites would triumph in overthrowing their enemies. Note, however, that victory is not ascribed to superior force of arms or battle skills: it is God, rather than Israel, who is the warrior, and

God fights with weapons that are not made from iron and steel (Ephesians 6:10–12).

Jesus has told us to love our enemies (Matthew 5:44–45), so we can no longer simply rejoice in their defeat. Rather, we invite them to participate in the salvation that has been given to us. The 'seder' contains a hint of this when participants shake ten drops of wine on to their plates to remember the ten plagues visited on the Egyptians and the many innocent people who died in them.

### Reflection

*Our salvation is not a licence for us to gloat over the destruction of others.*

VZ

# Salvation means a Saviour

The people who walked in darkness have seen a great light; those who lived in a land of deep darkness—on them light has shined. You have multiplied the nation, you have increased its joy; they rejoice before you as with joy at the harvest, as people exult when dividing plunder. For the yoke of their burden, and the bar across their shoulders, the rod of their oppressor, you have broken as on the day of Midian. For all the boots of the tramping warriors and all the garments rolled in blood shall be burned as fuel for the fire. For a child has been born for us, a son given to us; authority rests upon his shoulders; and he is named Wonderful Counsellor, Mighty God, Everlasting Father, Prince of Peace.

From the exodus onwards, God's people had many times of darkness: the splitting of the kingdom under Solomon's successors; the fall of the northern kingdom of Israel at the hands of the Assyrians; the fall of the southern kingdom of Judah, including the temple, at the hands of the Babylonians; the exile in Babylon; the hardships of returning and trying to rebuild Jerusalem. Then there were times of famine, plague and great economic inequality, and times when the people turned to pagan religion, abandoning their worship of the one God. All these are recorded by the historians and prophets of the Old Testament and it is not an encouraging story.

Now and then, however, the light breaks through the darkness and we get a glimpse of joy and peace that has not yet come, but will surely arrive. This is one such glimpse, quoted by Matthew (4:12–16) in relation to Jesus.

Salvation, in this description, is not only the coming of light into darkness or the defeat of enemies and the prosperity of God's people: it is a person, one who brings wisdom, power, parental care and, above all, peace.

'Jesus saves' is an easy slogan and easily parodied (Jesus the goalkeeper!). We will not fully understand it unless we fully understand the two words in it. Today's reading gives us a 3D vision of who Jesus is: wise, powerful, fatherly, a bringer of peace. Tomorrow's will give us a 3D vision of what salvation is.

### Reflection

*If an action doesn't serve peace, can it be of Christ?*

VZ

# Salvation is social

In days to come the mountain of the Lord's house shall be established as the highest of the mountains, and shall be raised up above the hills. Peoples shall stream to it, and many nations shall come and say: 'Come, let us go up to the mountain of the Lord, to the house of the God of Jacob; that he may teach us his ways and that we may walk in his paths.' For out of Zion shall go forth instruction, and the word of the Lord from Jerusalem. He shall judge between many peoples, and shall arbitrate between strong nations far away; they shall beat their swords into ploughshares, and their spears into pruning-hooks; nation shall not lift up sword against nation, neither shall they learn war any more; but they shall all sit under their own vines and under their own fig trees, and no one shall make them afraid; for the mouth of the Lord of hosts has spoken.

'I will not rest from mental fight, / Nor shall my sword sleep in my hand, / Till we have built Jerusalem / In England's green and pleasant land.' Blake's poem, set to music by Parry, is the song of the Women's Institute and also my school song. His vision of a new world, coming not 'in some heaven, light years away' (Marty Haugen) but on this earth, could have been inspired by Micah's vision.

What a contrast today's passage is to our first salvation reading, about the Exodus. Instead of victory in battle, we have the weapons of battle being remodelled into agricultural tools, the military academies being closed down, each family with its own home and food supply and fear banished from the world. We are a long way yet from that!

This classic Hebrew poem does not use the word 'salvation', yet the concept runs right through it. It tells us that salvation is not about 'saving souls from this wicked world', but transforming the wicked world itself.

Political leaders often use phrases such as 'a new world order', but their visions are never more than partly realized. Micah's vision, though (also in Isaiah), is of a truly new world and new people to inhabit it. It is promised not by politicians, but by God.

## Prayer

*Make us into people ready for your new creation.*

VZ

# Salvation is personal

He [Jesus] began to speak, and taught them, saying: 'Blessed are the poor in spirit, for theirs is the kingdom of heaven. Blessed are those who mourn, for they will be comforted. Blessed are the meek, for they will inherit the earth. Blessed are those who hunger and thirst for righteousness, for they will be filled. Blessed are the merciful, for they will receive mercy. Blessed are the pure in heart, for they will see God. Blessed are the peacemakers, for they will be called children of God. Blessed are those who are persecuted for righteousness' sake, for theirs is the kingdom of heaven.'

If I were a betting woman (in fact, I have never even bought a Lottery ticket), I would bet that you have been taught that the Beatitudes are about discipleship, not that they are about salvation. Perhaps you have heard them called the 'be-attitudes', as they tell us how to be.

It was at least 20 years into my Christian life before I heard someone point out the obvious: that this teaching is not a prescription, but a description. Jesus is not telling anyone to be poor in spirit, to mourn, to long for justice (a better translation than 'righteousness'). He is talking to people who already are downhearted, bereaved, diffident—people who long for justice because they don't have it. These are the people who belong in the kingdom of God.

To many of Jesus' listeners, the sign of God's blessing on a person was that they had wealth, high social status, perhaps military victory. To suggest that the lost and least in society were, in fact, the most important in God's kingdom was scandalous. It is entirely in line with the rest of Jesus' teaching, however—about the last being first, the greatest being the servant. Luke's version of the Beatitudes (Luke 6:20ff) makes this clearer by his parallel 'woes' on those who are rich, well fed, comfortable.

That is why I think this passage is about salvation; because it shows that God's greatest concern is to rescue the weak and powerless. If our concern is the same, it will bring persecution, because it will mean standing against the bastions of the world's power.

### Reflection

*'Follow me, and I will make you fish for people' (Matthew 4:19). Are these words only about evangelism?*

VZ

# How?

Since the law has only a shadow of the good things to come and not the true form of these realities, it can never, by the same sacrifices that are continually offered year after year, make perfect those who approach... For it is impossible for the blood of bulls and goats to take away sins. Consequently, when Christ came into the world, he said, 'Sacrifices and offerings you have not desired, but a body you have prepared for me; in burnt-offerings and sin-offerings you have taken no pleasure. Then I said, "See, God, I have come to do your will, O God" (in the scroll of the book it is written of me).' ... And it is by God's will that we have been sanctified through the offering of the body of Jesus Christ once for all.

The film *Atonement* was shown in cinemas not long ago, to great acclaim. Probably everyone has taken some action in their life for which they wish they could atone, even if some have repressed the memory of it.

In recent years there have been long debates (often producing more heat than light) about exactly how Jesus' atonement for our sins 'works'. The model in Hebrews—of a blood sacrifice for sin—is thought by many to be the New Testament's primary understanding of atonement. Others emphasize alternative images in scripture, such as debts being cancelled, a death taking away legal obligations, victory over the power of sin.

Today is Yom Kippur, the Jewish Day of Atonement, when, in Old Testament times, as well as sacrifices, a 'scapegoat' was sent into the desert bearing the people's sins (Leviticus 16:3–10). With no temple, Jews no longer perform sacrifices, but still fast for the most solemn day in their religious year (and then go to their friends for a slap-up meal!).

The writer of Hebrews tells us that nothing we can do will actually remove our propensity to sin. Only God's reconciling work in Christ can do that. We don't really need to know how it works, only that, if we give ourselves body and soul to Jesus, our sins are forgiven and we can begin our transformation into Christ-like people. That is salvation.

### Prayer

*'See, God, I have come to do your will.'* The prayer that Hebrews connects to Jesus can also be our prayer.

VZ

# Sin no more?

If we say that we have no sin, we deceive ourselves, and the truth is not in us. If we confess our sins, he who is faithful and just will forgive us our sins and cleanse us from all unrighteousness… My little children, I am writing these things to you so that you may not sin. But if anyone does sin, we have an advocate with the Father, Jesus Christ the righteous; and he is the atoning sacrifice for our sins, and not for ours only but also for the sins of the whole world.

A friend of mine, a fairly new Christian, was uncertain about being baptized. Some of her family were Jehovah's Witnesses and she had been taught by them that any sins committed after baptism could not be forgiven. Christians, too, have sometimes taught this, based perhaps on a distorted reading of later passages in 1 John (for example 3:6–9) and Hebrews (see 10:26–27). To refute this, here John talks to fellow believers specifically about confessing our sins and being cleansed of them.

Of course, even as Christians, we remain fallible human beings who will, at times, fall into wrong-doing. The difference is in our general attitude and desires. As followers of Jesus, we will 'abide' in him (John 15:4; 1 John 2:28; 3:9) and no longer 'abide in death' (3:14).

Imagine a person who emigrates to another country, where the customs and laws are different from those in their home country. At first, everything will be very strange and the immigrant will often lapse into the habits of the old country. After many years, the ways of the new country will have become second nature, because of the long time the person has lived there. It will only happen, however, if the immigrant is really committed to the values of the new country and wants to follow them. (Of course, in real life, immigrants are often right to keep some of their own customs.)

We, as followers of Jesus, have entered the new country of God's kingdom. It may take years for us to learn its ways, but we have the Holy Spirit as our reliable guide and tutor to help us make the change.

### Reflection

*'Little children, let no one deceive you. Everyone who does what is right is righteous, just as he is righteous' (1 John 3:7).*

VZ

# Salvation is a process

The creation waits with eager longing for the revealing of the children of God; for the creation was subjected to futility, not of its own will but by the will of the one who subjected it, in hope that the creation itself will be set free from its bondage to decay and will obtain the freedom of the glory of the children of God. We know that the whole creation has been groaning in labour pains until now; and not only the creation, but we ourselves, who have the first fruits of the Spirit, groan inwardly while we wait for adoption, the redemption of our bodies. For in hope we were saved. Now hope that is seen is not hope. For who hopes for what is seen? But if we hope for what we do not see, we wait for it with patience.

A visitor was admiring an old man's immaculate garden. 'Isn't God's creation wonderful!' she enthused. 'Ah,' replied the old gardener, 'but you should have seen what a state it was in when God had it to himself.'

Out of God's overflowing generosity, God has chosen that the world cannot be redeemed without the cooperation of human beings. Indeed, his choice that this should be so goes back beyond the entrance of sin into the world: Genesis 1:28 suggests that it is built into the very nature of creation to need human beings to manage it. We do not have a right to exploit nature so much as a duty to keep its balance.

In this passage from Romans, Paul tells us that salvation is not about saving souls separately from the world, but saving the world through the material actions of saved people. A task like this cannot be done instantly. Once we have given our lives to Jesus, we are, in a sense, both saved and not yet saved. Acts 2:47 puts it like this: 'Day by day the Lord added to their number those who were being saved.'

An old Amish man was asked by an earnest evangelical, 'Are you saved?' 'You see my neighbour over there?' he answered. 'He'll tell you whether I'm saved.'

### Reflection

*'Work out your own salvation with fear and trembling; for it is God who is at work in you, enabling you both to will and to work for his good pleasure'* (Philippians 2:12–13).

*VZ*

# Jesus' friends

In our culture we define 'friendship' in terms of affection. Friends are people we like and, during our lives, some friendships deepen, some fade and others simmer along on a low heat for decades. The biblical concept of friendship was rather different, though. It was defined by action rather than emotion and was a very serious commitment.

Abraham was known as a friend of God (2 Chronicles 20:7) and that kind of friendship was much closer to what we would call 'blood brothers'. In his culture, if your friend was in trouble, you fought, and maybe died, beside him. If necessary, you died in your friend's place. There was an ancient proverb in the Near East that summed up that kind of friendship: 'Blood is thicker than milk.' It meant that the chosen friend (the blood brother) was closer than a birth brother (who had shared the same mother's milk). That's why Abraham's tribal neighbours were nervous about his friendship with God—they understood that if they opposed Abraham, then God, his friend, would oppose them.

In the New Testament, because we read of Jesus' love for certain people, we think of them as his friends. Jesus' offer of friendship is more than affection, however, and in it lies an ancient truth, which is at the heart of the gospel. If Jesus is your friend and you are in trouble, he will fight (and die) on your behalf and, if necessary, in your place (John 15:13: 'Greater love has no one than this, to lay down one's life for one's friends'). God's love for humanity is defined by action, rather than emotion (Romans 5:8: 'But God demonstrates his own love for us in this: While we were still sinners, Christ died for us').

If we define friendship with Jesus by our contemporary concept of affection, then some people will grow deeper in their relationship with him, some drift away and others simmer along on a low heat for decades. If that sounds familiar, it means that the kind of friendship Jesus offers has yet to be understood.

For the next two weeks, we shall look at what a 'biblical' friendship with Jesus means. We shall meet holy people, rogues, disciples and outcasts, but they all have two things in common: they were all Jesus' friends and, in one way or another, were just like we are.

*David Robertson*

# Peter

When they had finished eating, Jesus said to Simon Peter, 'Simon son of John, do you love me more than these?' 'Yes, Lord,' he said, 'you know that I love you.' Jesus said, 'Feed my lambs.' Again Jesus said, 'Simon son of John, do you love me?' He answered, 'Yes, Lord, you know that I love you.' Jesus said, 'Take care of my sheep.' The third time he said to him, 'Simon son of John, do you love me?' Peter was hurt because Jesus asked him the third time, 'Do you love me?' He said, 'Lord, you know all things; you know that I love you.' Jesus said, 'Feed my sheep.'

This conversation between Jesus and Peter has many different levels of meaning, but today we look at just one and ask, is friendship with Jesus enough? Doesn't he require more? Doesn't he demand love?

Poor Peter. He said that he would never betray Jesus, but he did. He said that he would stay beside Jesus no matter what, but he didn't. Here Jesus asks him twice, 'Do you *agapan* me?' The Greek word means love—sacrificial, self-giving love, friendship of the ancient, biblical kind. Both times, Peter answers honestly, 'You know that I *philein* you.' This Greek word means like—the kind of 'like' we feel when we don't know someone very well, but certainly like them.

When Jesus asks him the third time, he phrases it, 'Do you *philein* me?' and Peter is devastated. He has come to know himself only too well—no more empty boasting, just honesty. 'Lord,' he says, 'you know everything; you know what I can offer you, my *philein*.' And Jesus accepts it.

Now, here's a thought. Jesus Christ offers friendship of the ancient kind, where he lays down his life for his friends, so, doesn't he demand the same kind of self-giving love in return? Well, it's the hallmark of love that it gives without expectation of return, so Jesus gives himself in love to Peter and to everyone—to us—regardless. If we are honest with ourselves, and with him, he begins a work in our lives where we are, not where we think we should be.

### Prayer

*Lord, I like you. Teach me
to love you.*

DR

# Nicodemus

Later, Joseph of Arimathea asked Pilate for the body of Jesus. Now Joseph was a disciple of Jesus, but secretly because he feared the Jewish leaders. With Pilate's permission, he came and took the body away. He was accompanied by Nicodemus, the man who earlier had visited Jesus at night. Nicodemus brought a mixture of myrrh and aloes, about seventy-five pounds. Taking Jesus' body, the two of them wrapped it, with the spices, in strips of linen. This was in accordance with Jewish burial customs.

We meet Nicodemus first in the third chapter of John's Gospel. He is a Pharisee, a member of the government and an important man, so he visited Jesus by night lest he be seen. It is clear that he didn't understand Jesus' words then and balked at the idea of being 'born again'. We should, however, remember that, at this point, Nicodemus was struggling along with no more than his own intellect. The Holy Spirit would not come until Pentecost and, without that inner witness, would any of us fare any better?

In John 7 (v. 50) we meet Nicodemus again. He tried to stand up for Jesus in the ruling council. He had much to lose and chose to remain discreet about his association with the rabbi from Nazareth. In contrast, Peter and the other disciples followed Jesus in the clear light of day. They stood with him— until the crucifixion when everything changed. Then they fled from the authorities and hid behind closed doors (20:19). That is when Nicodemus stepped forward, regardless of the consequences. When he claimed and buried Jesus' body, he proclaimed his allegiance.

A crisis tends to reveal what's in our hearts, which may not be the same as what's on our lips. When a Christian friend of our family suffered a heart attack, he was visited by numerous friends, and most of the Christians prayed with him and for him. Interestingly, it was his unbelieving friends who paid his car tax, mowed his lawn and ferried his wife and children around.

The friends of Jesus are not always 'high-profile' disciples such as Peter. They can be the 'low-profile' Nicodemuses who simply get on with the practical jobs that need to be done (Matthew 25:31–46).

### Prayer

*Lord, may my friendship with you be both real and practical.*

DR

# Lazarus

Now a man named Lazarus was sick. He was from Bethany, the village of Mary and her sister Martha. This Mary, whose brother Lazarus now lay sick, was the same one who poured perfume on the Lord and wiped his feet with her hair. So the sisters sent word to Jesus, 'Lord, the one you love is sick.' When he heard this, Jesus said, 'This sickness will not end in death. No, it is for God's glory so that God's Son may be glorified through it.' Jesus loved Martha and her sister and Lazarus. Yet when he heard that Lazarus was sick, he stayed where he was two more days.

Lazarus, Martha and Mary were Jesus' friends, yet, when he heard of Lazarus' illness, Jesus promptly stayed where he was! While the sisters waited for Jesus, their brother died. As we read on, we learn that Jesus raised Lazarus from the dead. The lesson is there to be learned: Jesus is the lord of life.

Surely, though, he could just have gone straight away and healed his friend? Yes, he could, so why did he stay away? Because he served God, his Father, not his friends. Jesus only ever acted according to the will of his Father (John 5:19–21) and so he waited for the right time—God's time—to act.

This can challenge our ideas. If we think friendship means 'special privilege', we may expect Jesus to make our lives easier. After all, if he's our friend, he should use his power to help us out, shouldn't he? Well, he always answers when we pray, but not in line with what we ask; he answers according to the will of God, the Father, and that may differ somewhat from what we had in mind.

So, why would anyone want to be friends with Jesus? Because he is the Lord of life and, if we seek life for ourselves and others, then the friendship he offers is our only choice (John 6:67–68). He's not a friend who does what we ask out of friendship; he's a friend who tells the truth and, the longer we know him, the more we understand of the will of the Father and our prayers become closer to his heart.

### Prayer

*Lord, thank you for your friendship.*

*DR*

# Mary

Six days before the Passover, Jesus came to Bethany, where Lazarus lived, whom Jesus had raised from the dead. Here a dinner was given in Jesus' honour. Martha served, while Lazarus was among those reclining at the table with him. Then Mary took about a pint of pure nard, an expensive perfume; she poured it on Jesus' feet and wiped his feet with her hair. And the house was filled with the fragrance of the perfume. But one of his disciples, Judas Iscariot, who was later to betray him, objected... 'Leave her alone,' Jesus replied. 'It was intended that she should save this perfume for the day of my burial.'

Celebrity isn't a modern invention and neither is social climbing. Lazarus was a celebrity and so was Jesus. What an honour it must have been to be invited to dine with the man who had been raised from death and the man who had raised him! The guests must have been on cloud nine—this dinner would be the talk of Bethany, and so would they To complete the evening, Lazarus' sisters were serving—except that Martha was, and Mary wasn't. Suddenly she was down on her knees, slopping perfume on to Jesus' feet and using her hair as a cloth.

It's one of those terrible party moments when, as if by mutual agreement, everyone stops talking, except for some poor soul who says or does something indescribably inappropriate. In the ensuing silence, the ceiling becomes strangely fascinating.

On this occasion, Judas broke the embarrassment: 'Why wasn't this perfume sold and the money given to the poor? It was worth a year's wages' (v. 5). What a relief, someone has said something! Now the guests could talk about the poor or charity or the cost of perfume or wages. The dinner was back on track and they could ignore Mary—until Jesus defended her. He accepted her gift and proclaimed that she was anointing him for burial. Try tucking into the pudding after that!

Jesus, like any celebrity, attracted fans, but fans are not friends. His friends were people who put him before social convention; they still are. Jesus, for his part, had a habit of ignoring the fans and concentrating on friends; he still does.

### Prayer

*Lord, whatever others might think,*
*I offer you my friendship.*

DR

# Martha

As Jesus and his disciples were on their way, he came to a village where a woman named Martha opened her home to him. She had a sister called Mary, who sat at the Lord's feet listening to what he said. But Martha was distracted by all the preparations that had to be made. She came to him and asked, 'Lord, don't you care that my sister has left me to do the work by myself? Tell her to help me!' 'Martha, Martha,' the Lord answered, 'you are worried and upset about many things, but only one thing is needed. Mary has chosen what is better, and it will not be taken away from her.'

Did this visit take place before or after the dinner at Bethany? It's probably a mistake to try to merge Luke and John's Gospels because all we end up with is speculation. It's better to accept their different accounts as presented.

Whenever this visit happened, the characters of the two women are clear. At the dinner party, Martha served and Mary didn't, and here it's just the same. Mary sits formally at Jesus' feet (the position of a respectful child when their teacher is speaking) while Martha buzzes about preparing the meal. Both, in their own ways, are serving Jesus and, at this point, he doesn't comment on their chosen roles.

Poor Martha. She probably wanted to prepare a really special meal for her friend and where was Mary? Skiving! We can almost hear the rattle of pots getting louder! Finally, exasperated with her sister, Martha complains and Jesus says what he thinks.

He compares Martha's friendship with Mary's. While Martha has allowed herself to be distracted by a plethora of preparations, Mary has concentrated on only one thing: Jesus. He is very kind, but the implication is clear: Martha, in trying to do so much for him, has ended up ignoring him, which is the wrong choice. The meal, like any other, will come and go, but he is the bread of life (John 6:35).

Friendship with Jesus is at his initiative, not ours (1 John 4:10) and we may need to let go of what we do for him if we are to find him.

### Prayer

*Lord, I'm so busy. Should I be?*

DR

# John

Early in the morning, Jesus stood on the shore, but the disciples did not realize that it was Jesus. He called out to them, 'Friends, haven't you any fish?' 'No,' they answered. He said, 'Throw your net on the right side of the boat and you will find some.' When they did, they were unable to haul the net in because of the large number of fish. Then the disciple whom Jesus loved said to Peter, 'It is the Lord!'... Jesus said to them, 'Come and have breakfast.' None of the disciples dared ask him, 'Who are you?' They knew it was the Lord.

According to tradition, the one described as the 'disciple whom Jesus loved' is believed to be John. He was one of three disciples whom Jesus chose as his companions at key times and John witnessed the raising of Jairus' daughter, the transfiguration and Jesus' final prayer in Gethsemane. The other disciples recognized this friendship and at the last supper they elected John to ask the question they feared to ask themselves: which of them would betray Jesus (John 13:21–25)?

So, John was not only a member of Jesus' inner circle but a singled-out member who was loved by the Lord. Why? Was it his temperament? He and his brother James were called *Boanerges* ('sons of thunder', Mark 3:17), so did his fierceness appeal to Jesus? Maybe, but *Boanerges* is an obscure Aramaic word and the meaning is unclear. What is clear is that, on the mountain of transfiguration and in the garden of Gethsemane, the only 'thundering' John did was snoring (and, as someone who tends to nod off, I sympathize).

Today's passage gives the only real clue as to why Jesus thought of John as a special friend. When none of the others recognized Jesus, John did. That recognition was spiritual, which is why, over breakfast, they 'knew' it was Jesus even though they weren't sure. If John was a man who could 'see' that, then he was a very special person, because that kind of sight comes only from a pure heart (Matthew 5:8). If John had a pure heart, it is natural that Jesus would have loved him for it.

### Prayer

*Lord, thank you that, by your grace, my heart is pure and, by your Spirit, I see.*

DR

# Mary Magdalene

Then the disciples went back to where they were staying. Now Mary stood outside the tomb crying... she turned around and saw Jesus standing there, but she did not realize that it was Jesus. He asked her, 'Woman, why are you crying? Who is it you are looking for?' Thinking he was the gardener, she said, 'Sir, if you have carried him away, tell me where you have put him, and I will get him.' Jesus said to her, 'Mary.' She turned towards him and cried out in Aramaic, 'Rabboni!' (which means 'Teacher').

What do we know about Mary? She was healed by Jesus and became a disciple, someone who followed and supported him. She stood by his cross (John 19:25) and was the first person to see him resurrected. She was also, probably, one of the women who prayed with the disciples before Pentecost (Acts 1:14) and a member of the church in Jerusalem, if not a leader, after the coming of the Holy Spirit.

We also know that she supported Jesus' ministry financially (Luke 8:2) and is mentioned in the same breath as Joanna, the wife of a wealthy man, so perhaps she was a wealthy woman. If she was, then she would be used to dealing with servants, which may be why her first thought on that resurrection morning was that she was talking to a gardener. She was, of course, talking to her friend, her teacher and her Lord: Jesus.

To our 21st-century eyes, this is the reward for her faithful friendship. She has stuck with Jesus to the end and beyond and now she is the first to see him risen from the dead. There is more to it than that, though. The religious teachers of the time interpreted old covenant law concerning witnesses (for example, Deuteronomy 17:6) to include 'miracles' and 'teachings'. Therefore, any work of God must be attested to by three male witnesses. Yet, when Jesus rose from death, the greatest miracle of all time, and the deepest teaching, was entrusted to just one witness—a woman.

When Jesus revealed himself to Mary, he wasn't only rewarding a friend but also proclaiming that, in the new covenant (as prophesied in Joel 2:28–29), everything would be different.

### Prayer

*Thank you, Lord, that you reveal yourself even to someone like me.*

DR

# The persecuted

Meanwhile, Saul was still breathing out murderous threats against the Lord's disciples. He went to the high priest and asked him for letters to the synagogues in Damascus, so that if he found any there who belonged to the Way, whether men or women, he might take them as prisoners to Jerusalem. As he neared Damascus on his journey, suddenly a light from heaven flashed around him. He fell to the ground and heard a voice say to him, 'Saul, Saul, why do you persecute me?' 'Who are you, Lord?' Saul asked. 'I am Jesus, whom you are persecuting,' he replied.

I think that this is one of the saddest moments in the Bible. Saul had been trained from birth to live a holy life and was destined to be a religious leader (Philippians 3:5). He had spent his whole life studying the scriptures, focused on knowing God, yet, on the road to Damascus, when he had the most significant religious experience of his life, when the light of heaven shone upon him and he met God face to face, he had only one question: 'Who are you?'

The people he was persecuting knew, though. They were men and women who had been 'cut to the heart' by Peter's words (Acts 2:37). The Spirit of God had spoken to them, they had turned away from their old lives, been baptized, joined the Church and shared a new kind of life together (vv. 42–47). They were friends of Jesus and Saul persecuted them for it.

These were not only people who knew Jesus but were known to him, personally. When Saul asked, 'Who are you?' Jesus didn't say, 'I am Jesus, and you're persecuting my people.' He said, 'I am Jesus, and you're persecuting *me*.'

The friendship between Jesus and his people was of the ancient kind—they were indistinguishable from each other. On the cross, Jesus laid down his life for his friends; he 'became' them (Romans 6:6) so that they might be forgiven and free. When they were persecuted, the hand raised against them was raised against Jesus as well.

Friendship with Jesus is no light thing, and neither is standing against it.

## Prayer

*Jesus, my friend, you died in my place; now I live for you.*

DR

LUKE 18:18–23 (TNIV)

# Choose your friends carefully

A certain ruler asked him, 'Good teacher, what must I do to inherit eternal life?' 'Why do you call me good?' Jesus answered. 'No one is good—except God alone. You know the commandments: "You shall not commit adultery, you shall not murder, you shall not steal, you shall not give false testimony, honour your father and mother".' 'All these I have kept since I was a boy,' he said. When Jesus heard this, he said to him, 'You still lack one thing. Sell everything you have and give to the poor, and you will have treasure in heaven. Then come, follow me.' When he heard this, he became very sad, because he was very wealthy.

When I was a boy, my two best friends were… let's call them Vic and Ray. My parents liked Vic, but they didn't like Ray. In fact, they thought he was a 'bad influence' because, when I was with him, I got into trouble. I think that, after all these years, I can now reveal the truth: the problem was actually me. Vic kept me on the straight and narrow, but Ray followed where I led—into all sorts of interesting situations.

The point is that friendship doesn't exist in a vacuum—it nestles within the context of other relationships. As teenagers, we may think that our friendships are private and outside our family life, but they aren't, because we aren't. If we haven't learned this by the time we grow up, we are in for some hard times, because trying to balance conflicting friendships and relationships can end up tearing us apart.

In today's reading, we meet a man who wanted to be friends with Jesus, the 'good teacher'. He was a righteous, honest man who tried to do the right thing, but his life already had a context and a central relationship. He already had a 'best friend'—money—and that friend governed his life: where he lived, how he lived, the people he knew, his self-image. When it came to the crunch, he couldn't give up that friendship, even for Jesus.

Being friends with Jesus always has a context. It impacts every other relationship, including our friendship with money (see Matthew 6:24).

### Prayer
*Lord, you gave everything for me;*
*I give everything to you.*

*DR*

PHILIPPIANS 3:7–9 (TNIV)

# Paul

But whatever were gains to me I now consider loss for the sake of Christ. What is more, I consider everything a loss because of the surpassing worth of knowing Christ Jesus my Lord, for whose sake I have lost all things. I consider them rubbish, that I may gain Christ and be found in him, not having a righteousness of my own that comes from the law, but that which is through faith in Christ—the righteousness that comes from God on the basis of faith.

Saul knew all about God, but did not truly know him until he met Jesus in that dramatic encounter on the Damascus road. From that moment, his life changed beyond recognition and, to make his new life clear, he took a new name: Paul. His blinded eyes were healed, he was baptized and began to learn about Jesus (Acts 9:17–19). He also began to preach and became one of the first missionaries to the Gentiles. Was it ironic or apposite that God should choose such a dyed-in-the-wool Hebrew to take Christianity to the non-Hebrew, multifaith world? Whichever it was, it was typical of God! For all the right reasons, God challenged Paul to change. He challenges us, too, offering us the chance to free ourselves from our past lives.

This is Paul's version of Jesus' call to the rich man in yesterday's passage, who was asked to leave behind that which he valued most: his money. Paul was asked to leave his own personal comfort zone (the religious practices that he understood inside out) and discuss his faith with people who did not accept his values in any shape or form.

Unlike the rich man, though, Paul understood and accepted God's call. He counted his old way of life as 'rubbish' compared to his new relationship with God (and it's worth noting that the NIV translation has toned down the original word when it uses 'rubbish'—the word Paul actually used was closer to 'manure'). What mattered to Paul was the 'purity', or 'savouriness', of his relationship with God through Jesus Christ.

Paul exchanged knowledge for friendship of the ancient kind. He no longer knew *about* God; because of Jesus, he knew God himself and was known by him.

### Prayer

*Lord, teach me your ways that I may know you.*

DR

# Zacchaeus

He [Zacchaeus] wanted to see who Jesus was, but because he was short he could not see over the crowd. So he ran ahead and climbed a sycamore-fig tree to see him, since Jesus was coming that way. When Jesus reached the spot, he looked up and said to him, 'Zacchaeus, come down immediately. I must stay at your house today.' So he came down at once and welcomed him gladly. All the people saw this and began to mutter, 'He has gone to be the guest of a sinner.' But Zacchaeus stood up and said to the Lord, 'Look, Lord! Here and now I give half of my possessions to the poor, and if I have cheated anybody out of anything, I will pay back four times the amount.'

Zacchaeus was a tax collector (the nearest equivalent we have today is probably a loan shark) who kept to the letter of the law while he broke it in spirit every single day. In most ways he was as different from the rich man in Monday's passage as he could be. That man was from a 'good family', socially acceptable and diligent about holiness. Zacchaeus, by contrast, was a thug who skated on the thin ice at the edge of the law and was widely recognized as a 'sinner'. In one fundamental way, though, both men were identical: they were united by a common friend—money.

To the astonishment of just about everyone, Jesus picked this tax collector out of the crowd. Zacchaeus, like Matthew before him (Matthew 9:9), was ready to change his life. The 'if' in his promise ('if I have cheated anybody') is a pretty big 'if'. Of course he'd cheated people—he'd cheated just about everybody! Once he had fulfilled his promise, his life was going to be very, very different.

When Zacchaeus met Jesus, he understood the choice before him: to be a friend of Jesus meant turning his back on his old friend money. Ironically, Zacchaeus the rogue had the courage to do what the 'righteous' ruler could not: give away most, if not all, of his wealth. There's a hymn that sums up his choice of friends: 'What a friend I have in Jesus'.

**Prayer**

*Lord, thank you for coming into my life—and for changing it.*

DR

# A friend in need

The teachers of the law and the Pharisees brought in a woman caught in adultery... and said to Jesus, 'Teacher, this woman was caught in the act of adultery. In the Law Moses commanded us to stone such women. Now what do you say?'... Jesus bent down and started to write on the ground with his finger. When they kept on questioning him, he straightened up and said to them, 'Let any one of you who is without sin be the first to throw a stone at her.' Again he stooped down and wrote on the ground. At this, those who heard began to go away... Jesus straightened up and asked her, 'Woman, where are they? Has no one condemned you?' 'No one, sir,' she said. 'Then neither do I condemn you,' Jesus declared. 'Go now and leave your life of sin.'

Those men hoped to put Jesus in an impossible position. Religious Jewish Law said that this woman should die, but secular Roman law regarded adultery as an entirely private matter and stoning in such circumstances counted as murder. Whatever decision Jesus made would get him into trouble. Jesus, however, focused on the disease (sin), not the symptom (adultery). Yes, the woman had sinned, she was a sinner, but what about everyone else? Were her accusers any better? No, and, when challenged, they slunk away.

In reality, there *was* someone qualified to pass sentence on the woman, someone without sin—Jesus (Hebrews 4:15)—but his response was to bend down and write in the sand. Was he killing time or working things out? According to the Law of Moses, the woman should have died. Could she be forgiven? How? The Law could not be ignored, but, if she was to be spared, who would die in her place? What of those other sinners—the teachers of the Law and the Pharisees? Who would die for them?

I can't help wondering if, when Jesus wrote in the sand, he was drawing a cross. The woman, of course, knew only that when she was seized by her enemies, Jesus was her friend. When others condemned her, he did not. She had no way of knowing that in order to free her, Jesus, her truest friend, condemned himself.

### Prayer

*Thank you, Lord, that you laid down your life for your friends.*

DR

# A friend indeed

Two other men, both criminals, were also led out with him to be executed... One of the criminals who hung there hurled insults at him: 'Aren't you the Messiah? Save yourself and us!' But the other criminal rebuked him. 'Don't you fear God,' he said, 'since you are under the same sentence? We are punished justly, for we are getting what our deeds deserve. But this man has done nothing wrong.' Then he said, 'Jesus, remember me when you come into your kingdom.' Jesus answered him, 'Truly I tell you, today you will be with me in paradise.'

It's all too easy to become overly familiar with, and blasé about, crucifixion; to think of it as a kind of firing squad or public hanging. Those executions, however, are over in seconds or minutes; crucifixion could last for days and there was plenty of time for taunting, cruelty and torture.

When Jesus hung on the cross, he was surrounded by all sorts of people, including spectators, priests, disciples and his mother (John 19:20–21, 25). Some came to hurl insults, others to weep; some (the soldiers) were there because it was their duty and others (the two criminals beside him) had no choice.

After being scourged (Matthew 27:26), Jesus died in a matter of hours. The men crucified with him were not so 'lucky' and, before the end, their legs were broken to speed up their death (John 19:32). No wonder one of them was filled with rage. The other, by contrast, stood up for Jesus in the only way he could—with his words. A self-confessed sinner, he asked only that Jesus 'remember' him.

That's the 'gospel', the 'good news'. That's all there is. A sinner admitting his need, turning to Jesus and trusting him. Jesus does the rest, as, on the cross, he dies for the sins of everyone: the crowds who came to stare, the priests, the disciples, his mother, the soldiers and the criminals.

There is a saying, 'It's not what you know, it's who you know.' As he died beside Jesus, one criminal came to know the only friend who could promise paradise and, by his own death, deliver his promise: Jesus.

### Prayer
*Lord, I trust you with my life and with my death.*

DR

# Old what's-his-name

When they came to the other disciples, they saw a large crowd around them and the teachers of the law arguing with them... 'What are you arguing with them about?' [Jesus] asked. A man in the crowd answered, 'Teacher, I brought you my son, who is possessed by a spirit that has robbed him of speech. Whenever it seizes him, it throws him to the ground. He foams at the mouth, gnashes his teeth and becomes rigid. I asked your disciples to drive out the spirit, but they could not.'

Let's list the disciples: Peter, James, John; Matthew, Andrew; er, Philip, Thomas, Judas and um, oh yes, Bartholomew and er, Thaddaeus and... hang on, it's in Mark 3... of course! The *other* James and the *other* Simon!

We know very little about these last four disciples. On special occasions, such as the transfiguration (Mark 9:2–13), Jesus took Peter, James and John to the mountaintop where they saw a vision of God's glory. At the foot of the mountain, the others had a chance to shine, but they didn't even glimmer—they failed to heal a boy and ended up at the centre of an argument.

Yet, Bartholomew, Thaddaeus, the other James and the other Simon were with Jesus for three years because he chose them. If anyone qualified as 'friends', they did. After Judas' betrayal, they (just like their more famous colleagues) ran away before the crucifixion, met the risen Lord, were filled with the Spirit and became leaders of the Church. They did all that and we know virtually nothing about them!

That, of course, is the point. Christians can be famous for all the right reasons (their holy, godly lives) or all the wrong reasons (being idiots), but fame is a human commodity and means nothing to God. He isn't interested, even slightly. He already knows each of us intimately and his focus is on our innermost, hidden selves—what the Bible calls our 'heart'. That is what God sees, judges and accepts, which is why, for every Peter, James or John, there are millions of 'other Jameses' and 'other Simons'. They are just ordinary people whom Jesus knows as friends in the ancient, biblical sense —people like you and me.

### Prayer

*Lord, I'm humbled that you would count me as a friend.*

DR

# Exodus 15—19

Studies show that if a number of people witness a particular event, such as an accident or a crime, they will all remember it differently. The differences may be small—'he wore a blue cap'; 'no, it was turquoise'— or they may be major—'the red car ran into the white one'; 'it was the white car that ran into the red one'.

If all their recollections were written down as one narrative, it would be very confusing in places, with repetition and contradictions. That is rather what our chapters from Exodus are like. Many scholars believe that is because they were not originally written down as one narrative, but have been put together from four different sources, each with its own perspective and its own emphasis. Those sources developed over many centuries of Israel's life and were finally brought together in the first five books of the Bible—the Pentateuch —probably about 400BC.

The Yahwist tradition (J), which stems from writers reflecting on their history in the time of Solomon, refers to God as Yahweh and sees the king as important. The Elohistic tradition (E) calls God Elohim and comes from the northern kingdom, after the kingdom of David and Solomon split apart. Prophets are very important in that tradition. The Deuteronomistic tradition (D) began in the northern kingdom and is particularly concerned with the Law and the covenant. The Priestly tradition (P) came into being during the exile in Babylon, when the priests sought to help the people find meaning in their sufferings.

All this can sound complicated, but it is helpful to know that apparent inconsistencies are not caused by incompetence or bad editing, but reflect the richness and diversity of the traditions that brought these texts to us. Seen like that, such details give depth to the story and show how the people continued to reflect on the crucial events of their story over many generations.

The stories we will be reading are also very human, demonstrating that human nature has not changed a great deal. We still find freedom hard to cope with and look round for someone else to blame when things go wrong. We still find it difficult to go on trusting God when life is hard, even with the evidence of his past care for us fresh in our minds. The people of the exodus struggled with the same questions we struggle with today.

*Helen Julian CSF*

# The Lord is our God

Then Moses and the Israelites sang this song to the Lord: 'I will sing to the Lord, for he has triumphed gloriously; horse and rider he has thrown into the sea. The Lord is my strength and my might, and he has become my salvation; this is my God, and I will praise him, my father's God, and I will exalt him. The Lord is a warrior; the Lord is his name.'

This is the beginning of a triumphant song, usually known as the Song of Moses, in which the Israelites celebrate the crossing of the Red Sea and their escape from slavery in Egypt. Opinions vary widely as to the date of the song in its present form—from contemporary with the exodus itself, in the 12th century BC, to the time of the exile.

The first twelve verses may indeed be very old or incorporate material from the time of the exodus. The Song of Miriam (v. 21), which is identical to verse 1, may have been the original song, with Moses' song as an elaboration of it.

In their rejoicing, the people do not take all the glory for themselves. It is the Lord who 'has triumphed gloriously'. What Moses promised (14:14) when the people were in great fear—'the Lord will fight for you'—has been proved to be true. The people acknowledge that this is the God who has been with them through the generations—'my father's God' (15:2).

Sometimes it is the smallest words that give us important clues, and here it is the word 'for' in verse 1. In Hebrew, it usually introduces a reason, a justification, for worship—'I will sing to the Lord *because*…'. Scholars see this song in its final form as a hymn to be used in worship at one of the great feasts of the year—perhaps at the Passover, the enthronement of a king or at New Year, celebrating God's kingship in the harvest.

Sometimes we come to worship with heavy hearts, feeling that there is little reason to be joyful or thankful. At these times, we can look back to our history, personal and communal, and find ourselves impelled to worship by what God has done for us.

## Reflection

*As you come to worship, why do you want to 'sing to the Lord'?*

HJ CSF

# We are God's people

'In your steadfast love you led the people whom you redeemed; you guided them by your strength to your holy abode. The peoples heard, they trembled; pangs seized the inhabitants of Philistia. Then the chiefs of Edom were dismayed; trembling seized the leaders of Moab; all the inhabitants of Canaan melted away. Terror and dread fell upon them; by the might of your arm, they became still as a stone until your people, O Lord, passed by, until the people whom you acquired passed by. You brought them in and planted them on the mountain of your own possession, the place, O Lord, that you made your abode, the sanctuary, O Lord, that your hands have established.'

This passage must have been written some years after the crossing of the Red Sea, as it covers the events that brought the people into the promised land. The list of peoples in verses 14–15—Philistia, Edom, Moab and Canaan—corresponds to the route of the exodus given in Deuteronomy 2:1–9, 18.

The author has used some poetic licence in writing this hymn, however. Although God's people did, in the end, occupy the land of Canaan, the existing inhabitants did not 'melt away' before them. It took about three centuries for the process to be completed. The chiefs of Edom do not seem to have been 'dismayed' as the people approached: Numbers 20:14–21 records that the Israelites had to journey around their kingdom.

The passage is written as theology rather than history. It is an expression of trust in the God who had redeemed them and continued to guide them on their journey to the promised land. He had chosen them, 'acquired' them (v. 16), had a plan for them and was with them on the journey. The words 'by your strength' in verse 13 are usually believed to refer to the Ark of the Covenant—the particular sign of God's presence among his people until they finally entered the land and established the sanctuary of God's presence in Jerusalem.

According to the covenant, God had agreed to be their God and they had agreed to be his people. Whatever happened, that was for certain.

### Prayer

*God of the covenant, help me to see your hand in all my journeyings and know myself to be yours.*

*HJ CSF*

EXODUS 15:22–25, 27 (NRSV)

# Complaining in the wilderness

Then Moses ordered Israel to set out from the Red Sea, and they went into the wilderness of Shur. They went for three days in the wilderness and found no water. When they came to Marah, they could not drink the water of Marah because it was bitter. That is why it was called Marah. And the people complained against Moses, saying, 'What shall we drink?' He cried out to the Lord; and the Lord showed him a piece of wood; he threw it into the water, and the water became sweet… Then they came to Elim, where there were twelve springs of water and seventy palm trees; and they camped there by the water.

We are still in the same chapter of the book of Exodus, but the whole tone has changed dramatically. Just three days into their journey (the period they had asked of Pharaoh so that they could worship God—see 3:18; 5:3), worship is the last thing on their minds. Perhaps it is not surprising. Water is essential for life and three days in the desert would soon have exhausted whatever supplies they had been able to bring with them in their hasty flight from Egypt.

Then they find water, but their hopes are dashed—it is bitter and impossible to drink. They turn on Moses and he turns to God, showing the dependence on God that has marked his part in this story. God does not let him down, supplying a means of making the water drinkable.

We don't know where Shur actually was. It is also referred to in 1 Samuel 15:7 and 27:8 and as Etham in Numbers 33:6–7. In the end, it doesn't matter much; the important thing is what the story shows us about human nature and the nature of God.

Our best and highest intentions are easily derailed by our basic human needs—for water, food and shelter. We so easily look around for someone to blame when we are in need. God, though, is faithful to his promises. He makes the water sweet and brings the people to Elim—an oasis where they can rest and gather their strength for the next stage of the journey.

### Reflection

*Do I believe that God will supply an oasis when I need it?*

HJ CSF

Exodus 16:1–3 (NRSV)

# Back to the fleshpots!

The whole congregation of the Israelites set out from Elim; and Israel came to the wilderness of Sin, which is between Elim and Sinai, on the fifteenth day of the second month after they had departed from the land of Egypt. The whole congregation of the Israelites complained against Moses and Aaron in the wilderness. The Israelites said to them, 'If only we had died by the hand of the Lord in the land of Egypt, when we sat by the fleshpots and ate our fill of bread; for you have brought us out into this wilderness to kill this whole assembly with hunger.'

The people have been on their way through the wilderness for perhaps six weeks, if we assume that they set off on the first day of the first month, but perhaps only for a month if they set off on the fifteenth day of the first month. It seems likely that they had not been on the move the whole time, though. Given the distances involved, they had probably made some quite long halts on the way.

Still, they are not happy. They seem to have learned little from God's help in treating the bitter water at Marah. Once again they are looking for someone to blame and Moses and Aaron, their leaders, are in the firing line. Although it is not long since they were crying out to God to rescue them from their slavery in Egypt, now that they have their freedom, they look back to Egypt with nostalgia. It seems unlikely that, in reality, they sat by the 'fleshpots' there. As

slaves they were probably given just enough food to keep them working, but, out in the desert, even that seems attractive.

I find this a powerful story about the fickleness of our desires. When a situation is pressing down on us, we ask to be freed from it. Once we have our freedom, we often find that it has its own difficulties, its own testing times, and we look back with nostalgia to our former condition. We forget the bad bits and remember only what wasn't so bad after all. Too often, we look around for someone to blame for the fact that we have what we desired.

### Reflection

*Can you recognize this pattern in your life now or in the past?*

HJ CSF

# Daily bread

The Lord spoke to Moses and said, 'I have heard the complaining of the Israelites; say to them, "At twilight you shall eat meat, and in the morning you shall have your fill of bread; then you shall know that I am the Lord your God."' In the evening quails came up and covered the camp; and in the morning there was a layer of dew around the camp. When the layer of dew lifted, there on the surface of the wilderness was a fine flaky substance, as fine as frost on the ground. When the Israelites saw it, they said to one another, 'What is it?' For they did not know what it was. Moses said to them, 'It is the bread that the Lord has given you to eat.'

Neither the quails nor the manna are miraculous in themselves. They are both natural to the Sinai peninsula. Quails migrate over the peninsula in very large flocks in spring and autumn. At night they alight to roost, when they are easily caught. Manna is composed of the secretions of particular insects. God, however, uses them to respond to the complaints of the people. Moses has reminded them (v. 8) that their complaint is really against the Lord. They see the glory of the Lord in a cloud over the wilderness (v. 10) and he has promised to provide for them.

The miracle is not in what is supplied, but in the quantities of both—available at the right time and in the right place. The people are even enabled to keep the sabbath by gathering double quantities on Friday (v. 5). It is very much 'daily bread' as whatever they each gather is enough for their needs for that day, but it does not keep until the next day, except on the sabbath, so every day the people must trust in God again.

God can use the ordinary to remind us of his provision for us and enable us to practise our trust in him and our obedience to his commandments. Like the Israelites, we often find it difficult to believe and need to keep testing, keep pushing the boundaries. Fortunately, God does not give up on us, any more than he gave up on his complaining people in the wilderness.

### Prayer

*God of the manna, help me to trust you for my daily bread.*

HJ CSF

# Remember, remember

The house of Israel called it manna; it was like coriander seed, white, and the taste of it was like wafers made with honey. Moses said, 'This is what the Lord has commanded: "Let an omer of it be kept throughout your generations, in order that they may see the food with which I fed you in the wilderness, when I brought you out of the land of Egypt."' And Moses said to Aaron, 'Take a jar, and put an omer of manna in it, and place it before the Lord, to be kept throughout your generations.' As the Lord commanded Moses, so Aaron placed it before the covenant, for safekeeping.

There is a lot about memory and memories in these stories of the wanderings in the wilderness. At times of crisis and times of joy, we naturally remember what brought us to this point. At funerals and weddings we tell family stories, look at photographs and say, 'Do you remember…?' Although for most of the stories will be familiar, for some it will be the first time they are heard—for the child, just old enough to be present; for the new in-law, learning what makes this family unique.

As we've seen, our memories can mislead us. The people soon forgot the reality of their lives of slavery in Egypt and remembered only that at least there was regular food. They forgot that they were not free to worship God. Once in the desert, they regularly forgot that God had supplied their basic needs in the past. Every time they became hungry or thirsty, they complained to Moses and became angry with him, so that, at one point, he even feared for his life (17:4).

Of course there were no photograph albums in ancient Israel, but the jar of manna, which was to be kept before the ark of the covenant, acted in the same way as a focus for memories and a starting point for stories. It was to be a reminder that God had fed them for 40 years in the wilderness—a whole generation—until they entered the promised land (16:35). When they visited the temple in later years, they could tell their children the story, too.

### Reflection

*How do you remember God's faithfulness to you? What is your 'jar of manna'?*

*HJ CSF*

# The prayers of the saints

Then Amalek came and fought with Israel at Rephidim. Moses said to Joshua, 'Choose some men for us and go out; fight with Amalek. Tomorrow I will stand on the top of the hill with the staff of God in my hand.'… Whenever Moses held up his hand, Israel prevailed; and whenever he lowered his hand, Amalek prevailed. But Moses' hands grew weary; so they took a stone and put it under him, and he sat on it. Aaron and Hur held up his hands, one on one side, and the other on the other side; so his hands were steady until the sun set. And Joshua defeated Amalek and his people with the sword.

The Amalekites and the Israelites were distant cousins, both groups descended from Abraham. The Amalekites are generally believed to have been a bedouin people, descendants of Esau, son of Isaac and grandson of Abraham. In the stories of the Judges and the reigns of Saul and David, they lived in the Negeb, in southern Judah. In this story, they are trying to prevent the Israelites from advancing into their territory.

Although just after these verses God promises to 'utterly blot out the remembrance of Amalek from under heaven' (v. 14), it was not in fact until the time of King Hezekiah, several centuries later, that they were finally defeated. It is one of the more uncomfortable aspects of the story of the chosen people, that other peoples had to be defeated and dispossessed in order for them to inherit their land.

This is also a powerful story of intercession. Joshua goes out to fight and Moses plays his part by praying in a very costly way for the entire day. He cannot maintain his prayer on his own, however, so Aaron and Hur (who appears only here and in Exodus 24:14) assist him in a very practical way, holding up his hands when he grows weary.

Today, many parts of the Church celebrate the feast of All Saints, remembering all God's saints— both the famous and the entirely unknown. For many Christians, the saints are not only examples of lives given to God but also intercessors in heaven on behalf of Christians still on earth. They raise their hands to God on our behalf and God hears them as he did Moses.

### Reflection
*Which saint particularly inspires you today?*

*HJ CSF*

# Sharing the burden

Moses sat as judge for the people, while the people stood around him from morning until evening... Moses' father-in-law said to him, 'What you are doing is not good. You will surely wear yourself out, both you and these people with you. For the task is too heavy for you; you cannot do it alone... You should represent the people before God, and... teach them the statutes and instructions and make known to them the way they are to go... You should also look for able men among all the people, men who fear God [and] are trustworthy... set such men over them as officers over thousands, hundreds, fifties and tens. Let them sit as judges for the people at all times; let them bring every important case to you, but decide every minor case themselves.'

Before the great encounter with God at Mount Sinai comes this story of human encounter. Earlier in chapter 18 we learn that Moses had sent his wife and her sons away. Now Jethro, her father, brings them back and there seems to be reconciliation (vv. 1–9).

Then the older man advises Moses on the practicalities of his relationship with the people he leads. Administration is often seen as unglamorous, and civil services and bureaucracies as boring. The decreasing number of people voting in elections, both national and local, bears witness to a sense that systems of government are of no interest to many people.

Here, Jethro, Moses' father-in-law, links the setting up of a system of devolved power with both Moses' own well-being and the people's relationship with God.

Moses is to represent the people before God and communicate God's commandments to them, but he is then to delegate much of the day-to-day work of administering the statutes and arbitrating in disputes to others, who are to have different levels of responsibility, depending on their ability.

Despite the grumbling of the people, some are now ready to share responsibility with Moses. Some have grown through their journeying and can share in the task of keeping the people faithful to their covenant with God and the proper use of their freedom. Perhaps administration isn't so boring after all.

**Prayer**

*Lord, help me to find my particular area of responsibility in your work.*

HJ CSF

# See what God has done

At the third new moon after the Israelites had gone out of the land of Egypt, on that very day, they came into the wilderness of Sinai. They had journeyed from Rephidim, entered the wilderness of Sinai, and camped in the wilderness; Israel camped there in front of the mountain. Then Moses went up to God; the Lord called to him from the mountain, saying, 'Thus you shall say to the house of Jacob, and tell the Israelites: You have seen what I did to the Egyptians, and how I bore you on eagles' wings and brought you to myself.'

The 'third new moon' is the first day of the third month and, with the new moon and the new month, there comes a new phase in their story. They have arrived at their initial goal—Sinai, the mountain of God—and they stay for some time. In fact, it is not until Numbers 10 that they set out again, nearly a year later. That is where God gives the law and where the tabernacle with the ark of the covenant is set up, as a sign of God's presence among his people.

Despite the fame of Sinai, there is in fact no certainty as to which mountain is meant, and commentators come to different conclusions from the evidence available. It is certainly in a wilderness area of some sort—not a comfortable place in which to spend nearly a year camped out. That, though, is where God keeps them as he teaches and instructs them, laying down the commandments and the fine detail of laws that should govern every aspect of their lives. It is also the place where the pattern of celebrations is laid down—the weekly sabbath and the festivals of unleavened bread, the first fruits and the harvest.

The basis for all this is, once again, the call to remember what God has already done for them. The demands that are made of them are a means of binding them to the God who has already bound himself to them and has carried them this far as an eagle carries its young (see Deuteronomy 32:11 for a vivid description).

## Reflection

*Do you have a way of reminding yourself regularly of what God has already done for you?*

HJ CSF

# Chosen to be holy

'Now therefore, if you obey my voice and keep my covenant, you shall be my treasured possession out of all the peoples. Indeed, the whole earth is mine, but you shall be for me a priestly kingdom and a holy nation...' So Moses came, summoned the elders of the people, and set before them all these words that the Lord had commanded him. The people all answered as one: 'Everything that the Lord has spoken we will do.'

The people have been rescued from slavery and brought to the place of meeting with God. Now God announces four ways in which, if they remain faithful to the relationship he holds out to them, they will be his chosen people. Each of those ways is rich in meaning and any one of them would provide much material for reflection on our own relationship with God.

They are to be his 'treasured possession'. They belong to him in a special way and are valuable to him. The Hebrew word is used in 1 Chronicles 29:3 and Ecclesiastes 2:8 to mean the king's private treasure.

They have been uniquely chosen 'out of all the peoples', but that choice was grounded in the fact that the whole earth belongs to God.

They are a kingdom of priests, a priestly people. Each has a right of direct access to the divine presence and, as a nation, they are to serve as priests for the rest of the world, representing them before God and seeking to bring them into relationship with the God who has called them. Isaiah 61:6 expresses the same idea; in the New Testament, it is found in 1 Peter 2:5, 9 and Revelation 1:6; 5:10 and 20:6.

Finally, they are to be a 'holy nation'. This is a unique phrase, used only here, although 'holy people' is used elsewhere, often with one of the other parts of this great litany of identity (see, for example, Deuteronomy 7:6; 14:2; 26:18–19 and, again, in 1 Peter 2:9). This draws on the root sense of 'holy' as something or somebody set apart—they are set apart from the other nations to worship and serve Yahweh.

Is it any wonder that the people eagerly agree to their part in the covenant, with such great promises being laid out before them?

### Reflection

*Which of these images is most powerful for you?*

HJ CSF

# Awesome God

When Moses had told the words of the people to the Lord, the Lord said to Moses: 'Go to the people and consecrate them today and tomorrow. Have them wash their clothes and prepare for the third day... You shall set limits for the people all around, saying, "Be careful not to go up the mountain or to touch the edge of it. Any who touch the mountain shall be put to death..."' On the morning of the third day there was thunder and lightning, as well as a thick cloud on the mountain, and a blast of a trumpet so loud that all the people who were in the camp trembled.

The God who has chosen the people, made them his treasured possession and called them to be holy and priests for the world, is also an awesome God. He is not to be approached casually or carelessly, but with careful preparation over a number of days.

In many cultures, this sense of the power of the sacred still survives. It is from these cultures that the notion of some things being 'taboo' comes. That which is sacred is also powerful and must be approached in the right way if its power is not to be destructive.

As Christians, we believe that Jesus has opened the way to God's presence through his death and resurrection and we can approach boldly. Perhaps, though, we also need to recover something of this sense of awe?

Certainly God can come very quietly and subtly, but sometimes his presence will be accompanied with thunder and lightning and make us tremble. In the Old Testament, such appearances of God are known as 'theophanies' and often associated with dramatic manifestations. The dramatic, in itself, is not a guarantee of God's presence, however. Remember Elijah on the mountain? For him, God did not come in the great wind or the earthquake or the fire, but in the 'sound of sheer silence' (I Kings 19:11–12). God chooses how he comes to each of us.

What is most important is not how he comes, but what he communicates when he does. Elijah was given his next commission for God's work. The Israelites, through Moses, were given the Ten commandments and the Law.

### Prayer

*Awesome God, may I be open to the many ways in which you come.*

*HJ CSF*

# Not in front of the children:
# 1 Corinthians 5—8

People often speak longingly about the experiences of the early Church. Corinth may not be quite what they are thinking of, however! Here was a church overflowing with spiritual gifts, tumultuous worship and outlandish behaviour. Paul's two letters to this young church indicate the depth of his challenge: how could he help them to live as Christians in a pagan society?

Our own society has many of the features of that pagan society. One obvious parallel is the extent to which our whole society has been sexualized. What was once thought to be obscene is now mainstream entertainment, advertising ruthlessly exploits desire in every form and pornography is big business.

Many Christians prefer not to think about these things, let alone talk about them. 'Not in front of the children' also means 'not in front of the Church'. Imagine what it must be like to become a Christian when you are from a non-Christian background. Suddenly the clamour that surrounds sex becomes a silence, only occasionally broken by rebuke and condemnation.

In the next few days, we are going to read about incest, homosexuality, marital relations and more. Why? Paul knew that these young Christians needed to know what was right and their new church needed to know how to deal with the whole range of sexual issues. Today, the Church worldwide still faces the challenge of helping new Christians live for Christ and express the positive fulfilment of God's gift of sexuality. It is not easy, but silence and avoidance are not acceptable alternatives.

We must also recognize the differences between our own society and that of ancient Corinth. Much of their expression of sexuality was linked explicitly with public religion, which means that we have to exercise great care in applying Paul's words to our contemporary situation. Misunderstanding these chapters can lead to abuse. That is one reason for choosing a modern translation for our chosen passages—the New Living Translation.

Chapters 5—8 from 1 Corinthians are not often read in church. They were written by a man desperate to keep a young and enthusiastic church moving in the right direction. My prayer is that his openness will speak to you.

*Stephen Rand*

1 CORINTHIANS 5:1–2, 4–5 (NLT)

# I don't believe it!

I can hardly believe the report about the sexual immorality going on among you—something that even pagans don't do. I am told that a man in your church is living in sin with his stepmother. You are so proud of yourselves, but you should be mourning in sorrow and shame. And you should remove this man from your fellowship... You must call a meeting of the church. I will be present with you in spirit, and so will the power of our Lord Jesus. Then you must throw this man out and hand him over to Satan so that his sinful nature will be destroyed and he himself will be saved on the day the Lord returns.

Paul simply cannot believe that people who call themselves Christians can behave like this. You probably know how he feels! I well remember preaching in a church that had just discovered their minister had resigned as a result of his sexual immorality. The congregation was in shock—they had known him for years and could hardly believe it.

I also remember an anguished conversation after the genocide in Rwanda. How was it that people who had shared Bible study could then kill each other with machetes? One argued that they simply could not have been real Christians. It is an awful reminder that all too often there is a gap between our words and our deeds.

We all suffer from that to some extent—but I hope we are still determined to narrow the gap as much as possible with God's help. Thank God that Jesus demonstrated a life with no gap between talk and walk. He alone can be trusted: ultimately our faith is not in our fellow Christians, but in Christ.

That does not mean public failings should be overlooked, however. They not only damage the Church's reputation but also dishonour Jesus and undermine the gospel. Paul insists that the church in question must separate itself from this particular person, who seems impervious to rebuke and correction. The final sentence is difficult; I think Paul is indicating that separating this man from the church ('excommunication') was best for the church *and* the individual. Some things just have to be dealt with.

### Prayer

*Father God, keep my conscience sensitive to your prompting and grant me your Spirit so that I can live with integrity and purity.*

SR

1 CORINTHIANS 5:6–8 (NLT)

# A little goes a long way

Your boasting about this is terrible. Don't you realize that this sin is like a little yeast that spreads through the whole batch of dough? Get rid of the old 'yeast' by removing this wicked person from among you. Then you will be like a fresh batch of dough made without yeast, which is what you really are. Christ, our Passover Lamb, has been sacrificed for us. So let us celebrate the festival, not with the old bread of wickedness and evil, but with the new bread of sincerity and truth.

Paul continues to explain why the church must act and distance itself from this individual who is openly flaunting his immorality. He uses an illustration that Jesus had also used, talking about the 'yeast' of the Pharisees and Sadducees (Matthew 16:11).

Failure to act would see the individual sin affect the whole church, just as yeast affects the whole loaf. If they removed that 'yeast', they would become like the unleavened ('unyeasted') bread of the Passover. They would then be able to genuinely share Communion together, with their sincerity and truth demonstrated by their determination not to tolerate impurity.

I can't help wondering if Paul was prompted more by shock at the reaction of the church than he was by shock at the brazen immorality on display. In yesterday's reading, he described them as proud; today he repeats the accusation by being appalled by their boasting—possibly about their willingness to be gracious and welcoming to the 'sinner'.

Paul's argument carries the ring of truth. I have known churches where adultery seemed to be infectious, creating a deeply twisted web of spiritual disease that crippled the life and witness of the whole congregation. There were spiritual battles to be fought and won if people were to be able to live in God's glorious freedom.

Sexual sin is no greater sin than any other type of failure to live in God's world God's way, but it can be devastatingly corrosive, destroying an individual's family and the church family. What a challenge to the church and its leadership, to find a way to deal with sin that recognizes its destructive force, but without becoming self-righteous, prurient and hypocritical!

**Prayer**

*Lord, grant wisdom and sensitivity, grace and conviction to those who lead your Church.*

*SR*

1 Corinthians 5:9–11 (NLT)

# Guilt by association

When I wrote to you before, I told you not to associate with people who indulge in sexual sin. But I wasn't talking about unbelievers who indulge in sexual sin, or are greedy, or cheat people, or worship idols. You would have to leave this world to avoid people like that. I meant that you are not to associate with anyone who claims to be a believer yet indulges in sexual sin, or is greedy, or worships idols, or is abusive, or is a drunkard, or cheats people. Don't even eat with such people.

I confess to being uncomfortable about these verses. History shows that church leaders too easily abuse their power. Church, which should be a place of welcome and peace, can end up as a place of manipulation, bullying and exclusiveness. You may know this from experience and I have met many people bruised by overbearing and malicious leaders. (I have also met leaders damaged beyond repair by vindictive church members.)

Yet, there is a clue here as to why Paul is so insistent on disassociation: 'I wasn't talking about unbelievers…' (v. 10). Jesus was known for eating with sinners, but they were people who made no pretence of being godly. Paul was as ready as Jesus to associate with anyone and everyone for the sake of demonstrating God's love.

Their rules were different, however, when it came to people who claimed to be followers of Jesus yet at the same time behaved with public disdain for God's standards.

Then, it was vital for the church to make it clear that it was impossible to continue fellowship (often expressed and experienced by the early Church as eating together) as if nothing was wrong.

There is real tension here. Christians who have taken these instructions so literally that they have refused to eat with their family have, I believe, done untold damage to the witness of the Church. So, too, however, have church leaders who have ignored inappropriate public behaviour. How do we demonstrate God's love and at the same time uphold God's standards?

Church leadership requires discernment, patience, firmness and a resistance to the temptations of power—qualities that can only come from a living relationship with God by the presence of his Spirit.

**Prayer**

*Lord, grant your Spirit's wisdom to all in church leadership.*

SR

1 CORINTHIANS 6:1–2, 4–6 (NLT)

# Settle out of court

When one of you has a dispute with another believer, how dare you file a lawsuit and ask a secular court to decide the matter instead of taking it to other believers! Don't you realize that someday we believers will judge the world? And since you are going to judge the world, can't you decide even these little things among yourselves?… If you have legal disputes about such matters, why go to outside judges who are not respected by the church? I am saying this to shame you. Isn't there anyone in all the church who is wise enough to decide these issues? But instead, one believer sues another—right in front of unbelievers!

Paul saw the Church as God's great prototype for a new society. It was made up of people whose relationships had been transformed—not only with God but also with other people, indeed the whole creation. So, imagine his frustration when people's attitudes and actions betrayed that vision.

It was even worse when the failure to live according to God's blueprint for human behaviour was openly paraded in front of the watching world. I remember one church secretary telling me that his church had been forced to give up door-to-door evangelism because the behaviour of two successive ministers had destroyed the credibility of the church with local residents.

Paul insisted that the law courts were not the place to settle disputes between Christians. Not only would public attention be drawn to the problem but also the judges would not be able to examine the case in the light of God's values. That's why it should be settled out of court and inside the church fellowship.

I once met a Christian who took this particularly seriously. His business was asked to do a specific job for the Christian organization I worked for. He produced a contract including a final clause that, in the event of a dispute, it should be settled by two Christians, agreed by both parties. He told me, 'I know I won't take fellow Christians to court, but I thought there should be seen to be a proper way to sort out a problem.' That is practical biblical wisdom.

## Reflection

*Our courts need Christian values and Christian lawyers, not Christians in dispute.*

SR

1 CORINTHIANS 6:9–11 (NLT)

# Kingdom people

Don't you realize that those who do wrong will not inherit the Kingdom of God? Don't fool yourselves. Those who indulge in sexual sin, or who worship idols, or commit adultery, or are male prostitutes, or practise homosexuality, or are thieves, or greedy people, or drunkards, or are abusive, or cheat people—none of these will inherit the Kingdom of God. Some of you were once like that. But you were cleansed; you were made holy; you were made right with God by calling on the name of the Lord Jesus Christ and by the Spirit of our God.

It is a tragedy for Christian witness today that homosexuality has become the issue by which so many in the Church judge the orthodoxy of fellow Christians, thus convincing those outside the Church that this is what Christians think matters most.

Verse 10 is often quoted in the debate. It is one of only four Bible verses—in most translations—that specifically refer to homosexuality, although Paul uses two obscure Greek words—translated here as 'male prostitutes, or practise homosexuality'—the precise meanings of which are extraordinarily difficult to establish.

What's more, when the Bible was written, there was no concept of homosexual orientation. So, applying these biblical texts to our contemporary situation requires care and humility, certainly not prejudice and homophobic bile. The biblical pattern of faithful, loving and joyful marriage must be upheld in a way that encourages and uplifts rather than condemning and excluding. God's love embraces all—and all are sinners, in need of God's love.

Here, Paul is emphasizing that our behaviour matters: 'Those who do wrong will not inherit the Kingdom of God' (v. 9). Those who *will* inherit the Kingdom will do so not because of what they have done, but because of what God has done for them—they are cleansed, made holy and made right with him (v. 11)—and who live lives that demonstrate God's transforming power.

### Reflection

*'Those who use and abuse each other, use and abuse sex, use and abuse the earth and everything in it, don't qualify as citizens in God's kingdom'* (vv. 9–10, THE MESSAGE). *Paul's concern is much broader than just sexual immorality.*

SR

1 CORINTHIANS 6:12–17 (NLT, ABRIDGED)

# True freedom

You say, 'I am allowed to do anything'—but not everything is good for you. And even though 'I am allowed to do anything,' I must not become a slave to anything. You say, 'Food was made for the stomach, and the stomach for food.'... But you can't say that our bodies were made for sexual immorality. They were made for the Lord, and the Lord cares about our bodies... Don't you realize that your bodies are actually parts of Christ? Should a man take his body, which is part of Christ, and join it to a prostitute? Never! And don't you realize that if a man joins himself to a prostitute, he becomes one body with her? For the Scriptures say, 'The two are united into one.' But the person who is joined to the Lord is one spirit with him.

'The truth will set you free' (John 8:32). The majority in our society, however, associate Christianity with restriction rather than freedom and many argue that the blame lies with Paul.

He faced a group of people within the early Church who believed that the result of knowing Christ and being set free from the power of sin was that a Christian could say, 'I am allowed to do anything' (v. 12) and live accordingly. So, Paul was constantly emphasizing that the freedom Christians enjoy is the freedom to live life to the full as God intended—that is, not the freedom to do as I like, but the freedom to do what God wants.

The members of a football team are free to kick the ball wherever they like, but the best possible game results from each playing according to the rules and follow-ing the manager's instructions. A cook is free to use any combination of ingredients, but the most satisfying results come when the cook follows the recipe.

The argument went further. Surely God is only concerned with spiritual realities. Thus, as the body is earthly, not heavenly, we can satisfy our body's appetite for sex just as we satisfy our stomach's appetite for food. God and morality don't come into it. Paul responds by stating a clear and powerful principle. A Christian is united with Christ as a whole person: spirit, mind—and body. Our relationship with Christ, therefore, is affected by what we do with—and to—our bodies.

**Prayer**

*Lord, grant me the freedom to live holy and wholly for you.*

SR

# Your body is a temple

Run from sexual sin! No other sin so clearly affects the body as this one does. For sexual immorality is a sin against your own body. Don't you realize that your body is the temple of the Holy Spirit, who lives in you and was given to you by God? You do not belong to yourself, for God bought you with a high price. So you must honour God with your body.

'Your body is the temple of the Holy Spirit' (v. 19). Here is the great mystery of the Christian faith. Just as Jesus was God incarnate, born in human form, so his Spirit is born in us. I grew up regularly being encouraged to give my life to Jesus. The good news is that, when we do that, God gives his life to us!

This is more than an individual reality. Paul's letter was written to a church and, in this chapter, all the pronouns are plural. This strongly suggests that the body Paul is thinking of is the Church, which is the body of Christ. In our Western tradition, we tend to individualize our faith, but Paul's consistent emphasis was on the way faith was worked out in God's new family, the Church.

When Jesus died, the temple curtain was torn open. Now God comes to us as individuals and builds us together into a new temple, a place of worship. The Church is not its buildings; it is a group of people born into a new family by God's Spirit and living a new life of worship, because God lives there by his Spirit.

So, Paul argues, sexual immorality abuses God because it is an abuse of our body, which is his body—individually and corporately. Sex is more than a bodily function—it links body, mind and spirit in a particular way; it links people together in a particular way.

Sexual immorality risks the physical consequences of unwanted pregnancy or sexually transmitted disease; it also risks the long-lasting emotional and spiritual consequences of broken relationships—with ourselves, other people and God. It tears families apart. All too often, it tears the family of the Church apart. Sadly, the evidence is all around us.

### Reflection

*The last sentence of today's reading could be translated, 'Therefore glorify God as a church.' Worshipping and working together without sexual immorality is one way to do this.*

SR

# Mutual fulfilment in marriage

Now regarding the questions you asked in your letter. Yes, it is good to live a celibate life. But because there is so much sexual immorality, each man should have his own wife, and each woman should have her own husband. The husband should fulfil his wife's sexual needs, and the wife should fulfil her husband's needs. The wife gives authority over her body to her husband, and the husband gives authority over his body to his wife. Do not deprive each other of sexual relations, unless you both agree to refrain from sexual intimacy for a limited time so you can give yourselves more completely to prayer. Afterward, you should come together again so that Satan won't be able to tempt you because of your lack of self-control. I say this as a concession, not as a command.

Verse 1 indicates that Paul is replying to a letter he has received and, in fact, he goes on to quote it. Sadly, our translation does not show this and, as a result, completely skews the meaning of these verses. The Corinthians had written, 'It is good to live a celibate life', which is not what Paul thought. He explicitly disagrees with the Corinthians' statement.

The original Greek literally says, 'It is good for a man not to touch a woman.' Some among the Corinthian church were so convinced that the body was dangerously unspiritual that it was best for married couples to abstain from sex in order to be more spiritual.

Paul responds by emphasizing not only that marriage is natural and good, but—radically and amazingly—it involves the mutual responsibility to satisfy each other's sexual needs. Husband and wife must equally give themselves to each other, because each belongs to the other. His 'concession'—that there might just be times when it is good to abstain briefly from sexual intimacy in order to focus more on God—is only acceptable if both partners agree.

Sex is not dirty or impure. Paul regards mutual sexual satisfaction as part of the normal purpose of marriage. Are you surprised Paul advocated that kind of equality for husbands and wives?

### Prayer

*Loving God, thank you for the gift of sex within marriage. May your Church demonstrate how sex can be enjoyed without abusing it.*

SR

1 Corinthians 7:7–9 (NLT)

# Single or married?

I wish everyone were single, just as I am. But God gives to some the gift of marriage, and to others the gift of singleness. So I say to those who aren't married and to widows—it's better to stay unmarried, just as I am. But if they can't control themselves, they should go ahead and marry. It's better to marry than to burn with lust.

Just a few verses—but very open to misinterpretation! It may be that Paul wished everyone was unmarried as he was. Indeed, later in the chapter we shall see him arguing that this has advantages in terms of being able to focus on God's work. Here, however, the Greek simply says, 'I wish that all were as I am', while the next verse emphasizes that marriage and singleness are both gifts from God.

It is just possible that Paul means the key is receiving God's gift and being content with it. In fact, the translation has again added to the original, which says, 'But each has a gift from God; one has this gift, another has that.'

Verse 7 may actually be the last part of yesterday's reading—those who are married should only adopt celibacy (for a short time) if they are sure that it is a gift from God. That would mean verse 8, addressed to those who aren't married and widows, is a new comment, not a continuation of the previous one.

For centuries, people have been too quick to jump to the conclusion that Paul thought marriage was a second best, a pandering to base instincts. Thus some commentators have argued that verses 8 and 9 are better understood as being addressed to widowers and widows, those who have been married. Whether or not that is true, Paul's emphasis seems to be that, if they haven't been given the gift of celibacy, then marriage is the right, good and natural option.

This topic will be extremely sensitive to some reading these words. Many, for example, experience singleness not as a gift, but a crushing disappointment. The emphasis in these verses is simply that marriage *and* singleness can both be gifts from God.

## Prayer

*Lord, grant all your people the grace to receive your gifts and trust you even when their deepest longings remain unfulfilled.*

SR

# Husbands and wives

But for those who are married, I have a command that comes not from me, but from the Lord. A wife must not leave her husband. But if she does leave him, let her remain single or else be reconciled to him. And the husband must not leave his wife… If a Christian man has a wife who is not a believer and she is willing to continue living with him, he must not leave her. And if a Christian woman has a husband who is not a believer and he is willing to continue living with her, she must not leave him. For the Christian wife brings holiness to her marriage, and the Christian husband brings holiness to his marriage… Don't you wives realize that your husbands might be saved because of you? And don't you husbands realize that your wives might be saved because of you?

Paul now turns to the challenges faced by married people in the church at Corinth. He states what he regards as the simple principle given by Jesus equally to wives and husbands: those who are married should not separate. No sooner has he reminded his readers of the Lord's command, however, than he goes on to give his own advice to those who have failed to keep it.

Marriage breakdown is painful. These verses are not easy, but there is no condemnation or legalism. The Church is not commanded to shun people in this situation. Church leaders have to honour their understanding of scripture and give genuine support to the people involved.

The Corinthians had another question. What if a husband or wife became a Christian and the spouse did not? First and foremost, the new believer should not seek separation. Paul wanted Christianity to be seen as a force that reinforced positive relationships, not an excuse to break them.

In principle, what God had done for an individual becoming a Christian was always stronger than any pagan force that remained in the marriage. In practice, the presence of the believing spouse created the possibility that God would bring the non-believing spouse to faith. For Paul, nothing could defeat God's power and nothing should stand against the mission of the Church.

### Prayer

*Pray for those wrestling with the challenge of marriage to a non-Christian.*

*SR*

# Freedom

Each of you should continue to live in whatever situation the Lord has placed you, and remain as you were when God first called you... it makes no difference whether or not a man has been circumcised. The important thing is to keep God's commandments... Are you a slave? Don't let that worry you—but if you get a chance to be free, take it. And remember, if you were a slave when the Lord called you, you are now free in the Lord. And if you were free when the Lord called you, you are now a slave of Christ. God paid a high price for you, so don't be enslaved by the world.

All of Paul's writings in these chapters are in a context that he is about to make explicit: 'For this world as we know it will soon pass away' (v. 31). Everything in the current social order will be changed by the return of Christ, so the greatest challenge is to live for Christ, whatever situation we are in.

The Greek word translated as 'continue to live' literally means 'walk'. They could be confident that, whether married or single, slave or free, Jew or Gentile, they could make progress, they could keep God's commandments. That confidence came from the fact that no social status, no situation, was beyond God's activity, because God had called them to himself in that situation.

Paul emphasizes that God's power is greater than the greatest social divisions. He was a Jew, a Pharisee, but now he was convinced that circumcision counted for nothing. Also, a slave might remain a slave in the eyes of society, but, in God's eyes, he was now free because God had bought his freedom.

These are not verses that justify Christians being unconcerned about injustice and modern slavery, as to turn a blind eye to these matters is indeed to be 'enslaved by the world' (v. 23). Rather, they remind us that God's freedom breaks through every human barrier. I recently heard of an Afghan woman who had become a Christian. She still wore a burkha—she had worn it since she was nine years old and did not feel comfortable without it—but, underneath it, she knew the freedom of Christ.

### Reflection

*How does God want you to use your freedom to live in the situation in which he has placed you?*

SR

1 CORINTHIANS 7:26–31 (NLT)

# The time is short

Because of the present crisis, I think it is best to remain as you are. If you have a wife, do not seek to end the marriage. If you do not have a wife, do not seek to get married. But if you do get married, it is not a sin... However, those who get married at this time will have troubles, and I am trying to spare you those problems... The time that remains is very short. So from now on, those with wives should not focus only on their marriage. Those who weep or who rejoice or who buy things should not be absorbed by their weeping or their joy or their possessions. Those who use the things of the world should not become attached to them. For this world as we know it will soon pass away.

This is a difficult passage, particularly if we try to apply it to our contemporary circumstances. It could be understood simply in the light of the final verse, which implies that Jesus will soon return and current normalities will all come to an end. Thus, it makes sense to suggest that no time and thought should be given to anything other than preparing for Christ's return. The problem with that is, some 2000 years later, Christ has yet to return: Paul's timing seems badly wrong.

However, the reading begins, 'Because of the present crisis...'. That suggests Paul was writing in response to a specific situation. Perhaps there was the beginning of a new outbreak of persecution. That would certainly mean the instructions would make more sense.

There is, perhaps, a general principle that can safely be taken from these words. In one sense, time is always short—and may be shorter than we think. Paul had an unshakeable confidence in the God who holds the future; he also had a passion for avoiding distractions and giving everything to God's service. Those are a great foundation for living life to the full.

It is possible to become so absorbed in things that are legitimate in themselves that we lose our spiritual perspective and passion for serving God. We get drawn into a society that invests its energy in things that do not last. We must always live anticipating eternity, but reckoning that time is short.

### Prayer

*Lord, keep us focused and passionate about serving you.*

SR

# Few distractions

I want you to be free from the concerns of this life. An unmarried man can spend his time doing the Lord's work and thinking how to please him. But a married man has to think about his earthly responsibilities and how to please his wife. His interests are divided. In the same way, a woman who is no longer married or has never been married can be devoted to the Lord and holy in body and in spirit. But a married woman has to think about her earthly responsibilities and how to please her husband. I am saying this for your benefit, not to place restrictions on you. I want you to do whatever will help you serve the Lord best, with as few distractions as possible.

Paul saw the world very much from his own perspective! He wishes people were like him—focused and not distracted—and, as an unmarried man, he seems to assume that marriage can only be a distraction and not a help in serving God. Perhaps he knew that his perspective was limited, which may explain why, several times in these chapters, Paul emphasizes that he is passing on his own wisdom rather than divine commands.

So his argument is, as THE MESSAGE puts it in verse 34, 'The time and energy that married people spend on caring for and nurturing each other, the unmarried can spend in becoming whole and holy instruments of God.' Paul is not against marriage, however. He insists that it is right for husbands and wives to be concerned about each other. Too many make the mistake of giving so much time to their church activities that they neglect their spouses. If you are married, your spouse is a gift from God with a legitimate expectation of your time and attention.

Once again, Paul emphasizes his radical understanding that those responsibilities apply equally to husbands and wives. There is no biblical basis here for the belief that wives are subordinate to their husbands—in the home, in the Church or in society at large.

A final thought. If the 'present crisis' in yesterday's reading was severe persecution, then there was undoubtedly added pressure for those with a family when following Jesus, as it could have meant imprisonment or death.

### Reflection

*How can I 'serve the Lord best, with as few distractions as possible'?*

SR

1 CORINTHIANS 7:36–40 (NLT)

# To marry or not to marry?

But if a man thinks that he's treating his fiancée improperly and will inevitably give in to his passion, let him marry her as he wishes. It is not a sin. But if he has decided firmly not to marry and there is no urgency and he can control his passion, he does well not to marry. So the person who marries his fiancée does well, and the person who doesn't marry does even better. A wife is bound to her husband as long as he lives. If her husband dies, she is free to marry anyone she wishes, but only if he loves the Lord. But in my opinion it would be better for her to stay single, and I think I am giving you counsel from God's Spirit when I say this.

Commentators are agreed: the first part of this passage is hard to translate and hard to understand! Paul seems to start by addressing the fiancé and then switches to the father of the bride. Our translation is an attempt to make coherent sense of the original, but it is not necessarily correct.

It does seem to reinforce the view that Paul commends being single *and* marriage, but prefers being single for the reasons we thought about yesterday. Note that this is because Paul sees the mission of the Church as the greatest priority, but then so should those who are married. Their life together, with or without children, is not an alternative to serving God or a barrier to serving him, but brings unique opportunities to do so. I can think of examples within my own family—the possibilities for hospitality, including overseas students gathered round a Christmas dinner table, becoming a parent governor, building lasting relationships with other mothers at the school gate.

The second part of today's reading returns to the situation of those who are widowed. They are free to marry, but Paul's advice is that, if they do, they should marry a Christian. This is consistent with the priority he gives to mission. I know many have struggled—painfully—to know whether or not they should marry a non-Christian. Part of the harsh reality is that it makes serving God together impossible and often makes it harder to serve God as an individual.

### Prayer

*Pray for those who long for marriage and struggle to find a Christian partner.*

SR

# Food for thought

Now regarding your question about food that has been offered to idols. Yes, we know that 'we all have knowledge' about this issue. But while knowledge makes us feel important, it is love that strengthens the church. Anyone who claims to know all the answers doesn't really know very much. But the person who loves God is the one whom God recognizes.

The letter from Corinth raised a wide variety of knotty, practical questions that were really important to the Christians there. So, Paul moves from sexual relationships and marriage to food offered to idols—a problem far removed from our experience.

Corinth was a typical city of the ancient world. Animals were offered as sacrifices in temples dedicated to various gods. The priests would eat some of the meat and the rest would be sold in the local shops. You might have been able to avoid buying it, but it would have been much harder to avoid eating had you participated in the normal social life of the city.

While the issue seems to lack any relevance to our situation, it raised very basic issues about how much Christians were free to participate in society as opposed to separating themselves from an evil world. Eating food offered to idols was a lifestyle issue.

In answering the Corinthians' question Paul states a principle that is incredibly relevant to all of us: love is what matters most. Christians now debate lifestyle issues such as smoking, drinking alcohol, what to do on Sundays, what to watch on television, how to raise children, pacifism—the list is almost endless. Whatever the topic, though, you may be sure that you know what is right. Knowing what is right is important—but not as important as love: loving God and loving his people.

The same applies to disagreements in church. Whether the hot topic in your church is the style of worship, the structure of leadership, the use of charismatic gifts or modernizing the building, the fact is that you are entitled to your opinion and your opinion matters. However, it doesn't matter as much as love—loving God and his people.

### Prayer

*Dear Lord, help me always to express my opinions in a way that is helpful and loving.*

SR

1 CORINTHIANS 8:4–8 (NLT, ABRIDGED)

# Only one God

So, what about eating meat that has been offered to idols? Well, we all know that an idol is not really a god and that... there is only one God, the Father, who created everything, and we live for him. And there is only one Lord, Jesus Christ, through whom God made everything and through whom we have been given life... Some are accustomed to thinking of idols as being real, so when they eat food that has been offered to idols, they think of it as the worship of real gods, and their weak consciences are violated. It's true that we can't win God's approval by what we eat. We don't lose anything if we don't eat it, and we don't gain anything if we do.

Paul continues to respond to the letter from Corinth. It seems that it had quoted their view 'that an idol is not really a god'. That triggered Paul into articulating a creed—a deeply theological statement of Christian truth.

The God that the Christians worshipped was not an idol. He was—and is—the only God. Idols are representations of gods that do not exist; God is the Father of all because he is the creator of all. Idols are made of material that has come from the hand of the creator God. He is also the sustainer of life. All life comes from him, which is why Christians live for him.

Then Paul moves from Jewish orthodoxy to the startlingly radical and offensive Christian confession that 'Jesus is Lord'. Offensive to the Jews because it appeared to be an additional God; offensive to the Romans because it meant using the title that Caesar had claimed as his own. This Lord, Jesus Christ (the Messiah), was not only responsible for the original creation, but also for the new life given to his followers: he was creator, redeemer, saviour, friend.

Some of the members of the Corinthian church were determined to celebrate the freedom that Jesus had brought them. Perhaps by actively seeking out and eating the meat offered to idols they would demonstrate their spirituality and move closer to God. Our lifestyle decisions don't earn God's approval, however—they must stem from the life God has given us in Christ.

### Prayer

*Loving God, thank you for making us; thank you for remaking us and giving us the life of Jesus.*

SR

# Thinking of others

But you must be careful so that your freedom does not cause others with a weaker conscience to stumble. For if others see you—with your 'superior knowledge'—eating in the temple of an idol, won't they be encouraged to violate their conscience by eating food that has been offered to an idol? So because of your superior knowledge, a weak believer for whom Christ died will be destroyed. And when you sin against other believers by encouraging them to do something they believe is wrong, you are sinning against Christ. So if what I eat causes another believer to sin, I will never eat meat again as long as I live—for I don't want to cause another believer to stumble.

It seems that some Corinthians were so sure of their freedom in Christ that they even felt able to attend pagan rituals. Their faith was so strong that they knew they would not be affected.

This behaviour provokes Paul to make a statement of principle. Whatever our certainties, he says, we must always think of the impact of our actions on others—that is the most important consideration. It is hard to emphasize enough the strength of Paul's language here. Deliberately—even thoughtlessly—to make life hard for other Christians is not just wrong, it is a sin against Christ. How can that be?

Paul believed that Christians belong to each other because every Christian belongs to Christ. If we are members together of the body of Christ, we don't just hurt a friend when we hurt another Christian. Our thoughtlessness hurts God. So, Paul refrains from something he has the freedom and every right to do because he is committed to building up, not tripping up, his fellow believers: 'Be humble, thinking of others as better than yourselves' (Philippians 2:3).

This is a good place to end these difficult, sometimes perplexing, readings. Sex, singleness and marriage are gifts from God, but can also cause great pain and complexity. Paul felt the bonds of his Christian family very deeply. He wrote as he did because he cared about the family of God and wanted to protect family relationships.

### Prayer

*Lord, thank you for making me part of your worldwide family. Help me to encourage and strengthen other members of your body. Amen*

SR

# Words of consolation and challenge

Mark Twain famously observed that it was not the bits of scripture he didn't understand that he found to be a problem, but those he did! For the words of consolation and challenge we shall be considering next, I have mostly chosen well-known pieces of scripture, ones where the meaning is obvious but the receiving and living out of that meaning is enormously difficult.

We will start with a challenge. Using words that come mainly from Jesus' Sermon on the Mount, we will explore what it means to, in doing that, we will inevitably be aware of our shortcomings and failings.

Bishop Morris Maddocks defined the healing ministry as 'Jesus Christ meeting you at the point of your deepest need'. The words of consolation that follow in the second week will meet us at the precise point where we find the challenge most difficult. For instance, Jesus challenges us to love our enemies as well as our friends (see Matthew 5:44). We know the importance of this as we are consoled by the fact that, when we were still sinners, still enemies of God and estranged from God's ways, Christ died for us (Romans 5:8). Thus, we will both see the height at which the bar is set—the enormous demands of the Christian life and the challenge of living in a Christ-like way—and experience the grace and tenderness of God as revealed to us in Christ.

In Chichester Cathedral, there is a lovely modern stained-glass window depicting the story of Peter walking across the water to Jesus. Halfway, his faith fails him and he starts to sink—'Lord, save me,' he cries out. In the window, Jesus reaches out to Peter. He has the most enormous arms, stretching out, embracing, lifting up. No matter how far we fall or how often we stumble or however many times we fail to meet the challenge, God reaches out to us in Christ to lift us up and carry us.

Our God shares our temptations and challenges. He knows what it's like to be human. God's love in Christ comes constantly to our aid, meeting us in our weakness and assisting us in the challenge of living a Christ-like life. All of us who follow Christ will experience challenge and consolation in equal measure. We need both, but let us also be sure: the final word is consolation.

*Stephen Cottrell*

MATTHEW 22:35–40 (NRSV)

# The greatest commandment

A lawyer asked him [Jesus] a question to test him. 'Teacher, which commandment in the law is the greatest?' He said to him, '"You shall love the Lord your God with all your heart, and with all your soul, and with all your mind." This is the greatest and first commandment. And a second is like it: "You shall love your neighbour as yourself." On these two commandments hang all the law and the prophets.'

Jesus sums up the whole law with the challenge that you must love God and love your neighbour as yourself. 'Do to others as you would have them do to you' (Matthew 7:12) is the commandment on which all Christian ethics are based. It requires us to stop viewing ourselves in isolation from God and each other.

If I want to be treated with generosity, consideration, mercy, then I must be generous, considerate and merciful to others. I cannot allow myself the luxury of imagining that my actions do not affect others. I cannot expect the world to be hospitable and forgiving if my heart burns with greed and envy. Thus it is that Jesus presents us with an uncomfortably practical way to order our lives. Every decision we make, every word we utter, every action we take, even every thought, must be considered and judged by its effect on others.

Our whole life is to be understood in relation to others. We are all part of one magnificent dance where love of God and love of neighbour draws us into new community and a deeper appreciation of the way in which our words and actions—large and small—shape the universe. My tap left running while I clean my teeth ultimately robs my brothers and sisters in Africa of water they need to drink. My television left on standby contributes to global warming. My ill-judged rebuke or that joke I made at someone else's expense set in motion a chain reaction of anger and now hundreds are hurting. My lack of penitence leaves God weeping.

### Prayer

*Merciful God, help me to love myself and receive and serve others with that same generosity that you show us in Christ—generosity that I long to receive myself.*

SC

# Going the extra mile

[Jesus said] 'You have heard that it was said, "You shall love your neighbour and hate your enemy." But I say to you, love your enemies and pray for those who persecute you, so that you may be children of your Father in heaven; for he makes his sun rise on the evil and on the good, and sends rain on the righteous and on the unrighteous. For if you love those who love you, what reward do you have? Do not even the tax-collectors do the same?'

As if loving our neighbour—just the people of our everyday encounters—wasn't enough, Jesus challenges us to go even further and deeper. He tells us that we must love our enemies as well. That is what we might call the extra mile of love. The first mile is that way of living where we deal with others in the way we would like to be dealt with ourselves. The extra mile involves extending that same generosity of love even to those who oppose us and despise us.

That sort of love is dangerously difficult—easy to put down in a few pious words, extraordinarily hard to live out, even for a few moments. When we do actually encounter someone whom we know to be our enemy, not only are we full of fear, pumped up with the adrenalin of hate and spite, but who among us does not also entertain thoughts of revenge?

It is in just such situations, where we dream of dominating and humbling an enemy, that Jesus asks us to reach out in service, to give our enemy a drink. Of course, that is also the ultimate humiliation for, as we humble ourselves before the person who despises us, so they are shamed by the steadfast tenacity of our love. It is the only way we shall ever build peace in our world. It will be painstakingly constructed from thousands of little acts of love to those from whom, at the moment, we are estranged. Yes, we should have bombed Iraq—but with food parcels and love letters.

### Prayer

*Generous God, you reach out to everyone through Christ. Help me to reach out to those who are my enemies and banish fear and hatred from my heart.*

*SC*

# Unclenching your fist

[Jesus said] 'You have heard that it was said, "An eye for an eye and a tooth for a tooth." But I say to you, do not resist an evildoer. But if anyone strikes you on the right cheek, turn the other also; and if anyone wants to sue you and take your coat, give your cloak as well; and if anyone forces you to go one mile, go also the second mile. Give to everyone who begs from you, and do not refuse anyone who wants to borrow from you.'

The challenge of Jesus' teaching gets harder and harder to take. The muttering and grumbles of disapproval among his audience increase. How can such idealistic dreaming have a place in the real world? So you might show a bit more consideration to your neighbour, but try giving your enemy something to eat and he will soon show you where to get off! Give your enemy a wide berth. Live a separate life. Keep out of trouble. That, surely, would be a far more sensible course of action.

Your enemy will seize on your weakness. He will not receive your gift with gratitude. Instead, he will most likely crush you. What then, Jesus? Wouldn't it have been better to have kept out of harm's way in the first place?

Jesus looks at us with steadfast love. He sees in our fear the very beginnings of the violence that made us enemies to begin with. He tells us that we must receive the violence on one cheek and then turn and offer the other.

I don't know how to do this. I can't imagine being able to confront violence with such graceful determination. I still believe that there are some situations where it is justifiable, as a last resort, to use force against those who crush the innocent. I also know, however, that most of the violence in the world just begets more violence. The real challenge is to find another way. The survival of our world depends on it.

### Prayer

*Vulnerable God, you brought peace by facing the violence of your enemies with the stubborn generosity of love. Change my heart and make it able to bear the torments and furies of the world. Only then will it be able to love.*

SC

MATTHEW 20:25–28 (NRSV)

# Learning to serve

Jesus called them [the disciples] to him and said, 'You know that the rulers of the Gentiles lord it over them, and their great ones are tyrants over them. It will not be so among you; but whoever wishes to be great among you must be your servant, and whoever wishes to be first among you must be your slave; just as the Son of Man came not to be served but to serve, and to give his life as a ransom for many.'

There is a startling story in Luke's Gospel about Jesus saying to his little flock of disciples that the Father wants to give them the Kingdom (see Luke 12:32). Jesus then says that they must be like those who are waiting up for their master to return. Their lamps must be constantly burning. They must remain awake and alert. So far, the story is familiar; Jesus often speaks about the need to be ready for action. This particular story has an astonishing twist, however. When the Master returns, it is not the ever-vigilant servants who will wait on him. Rather, he will 'fasten his belt and have them sit down to eat, and he will come and serve them' (v. 37).

Jesus models to his disciples a way of leadership and service that shames and contradicts the power games of the world. The first will be last; the one who wishes to be greatest must become a servant, as spelled out in today's passage. Such a way of living is a wonderful antidote to the feverish clamour for status, position and power that eats away at the human spirit.

Most of us spend most of our time looking for affirmation and recognition in all the wrong places. Yet, however the world rewards us, none of it lasts—even those things that are good and noble. In the end—and this is the disturbing insight of the Advent season that begins on Sunday—we stand before God. It is the knowledge that we are recognized by him, served by him and loved by him that is the only thing worth seeking. Then, with grateful hearts, we offer ourselves to others in humble service.

### Prayer

*Gracious God, foot washer, storm calmer, cross bearer, servant King, teach me your way of service.*

SC

# Sitting lightly to possessions

Jesus said to him [the rich young man], 'If you wish to be perfect, go, sell your possessions, and give the money to the poor, and you will have treasure in heaven; then come, follow me.' When the young man heard this word, he went away grieving, for he had many possessions.

Someone recently asked if they could come and talk to me about their spiritual life. I said I would be happy to see them and suggested they brought their latest credit card statement with them. They were slightly taken aback. Why did I want to discuss their credit card spending? I suggested it would be the surest indicator of where their true priorities lay.

The context of the passage is the story of a rich young man who keeps all the commandments, but can't accept the next challenge. He turns away, disconsolate. His wealth gets in the way of him following Jesus.

Speaking personally, I cannot read this story without feeling compromised and constrained by my own wealth. Even the poorest in Britain have great riches compared with millions of people in the world. Many of us throw away more food each week than others have to begin with. We've stopped letting this story scandalize us, though. We let ourselves off the hook. We talk about the importance of wealth creation, the relative nature of poverty, the responsibility of governments, but we don't have the moral courage to either walk away from Jesus because we cannot follow his teaching or make a real effort to conform our lives to his challenge. Following Jesus is not supposed to allow us treasure on earth. Jesus often speaks about giving up possessions, storing up treasure in heaven.

A proper sense of stewardship about our possessions is the one thing that many of us lack. We turn Jesus into our private life coach, available for help with issues of personal morality, but effectively barred from those places where his teaching might actually demand some radical change. So, what sort of treasure do you really want? The sort that glitters on earth and will win admiring glances from the world or the sort that lasts?

## Prayer

*Tenacious God, overcome the brutish persistence of self and open my account in heaven.*

*SC*

# Praying all the time

Rejoice always, pray without ceasing, give thanks in all circumstances; for this is the will of God in Christ Jesus for you.

This is a different sort of challenge, but it opens the doors to having some hope as far as all the others are concerned. It is about recognizing where my resources truly come from. Am I to see Christ as a wonderful and challenging example of how I should live (and then grit my teeth in steely determination and try to do the same) or can God actually help me? Can he help me be more generous? Can he give me a servant heart? Can he help me to go that extra mile? Can he enable me to love both my neighbour and my enemy? Can he help me to love myself? In other words, is Christ a role model or a saviour?

The Christian faith tells us that God is both. God shows me how to live my life, but also recognizes that at every step I am prone to stumble. So, he provides resources —overflowing streams of goodness and mercy—to shape and irrigate our lives and every action. We receive these resources through prayer. Not that prayer should be thought of primarily as a means of accessing resources from God— first of all it is about offering thanks to God—but it is also a way of discovering God's agenda for the world. When we pray, we align our will to God's.

Do that all the time, says Paul. Well, he doesn't actually mean 'do that activity we call prayer' all the time. He means that we should make our lives a prayer. Allow every thought and action to be shaped by God. Live in tune with God.

Doing so requires times of prayer. It requires discipline as well as desire. The challenge is to let those times be the well from which we draw resources for everything else. So, how come we always end up reckoning that we are too busy to pray? It's like saying we're too busy to breathe.

### Prayer

*Faithful God, discipline my desire and use the few moments of my attentive searching so that I am found by you. Sing your song of love in my heart and shape my life.*

*SC*

MATTHEW 7:1–3 (NRSV)

# Judgment belongs to God

[Jesus said] 'Do not judge, so that you may not be judged. For with the judgment you make you will be judged, and the measure you give will be the measure you get. Why do you see the speck in your neighbour's eye, but do not notice the log in your own eye?'

We are back to the Sermon on the Mount—that challenging summation of Jesus' teaching. We've seen what a citizen of God's kingdom looks like. We've acknowledged how far short of that ideal we fall. Now Jesus tells us that it is not our place to judge. That comes as a shock: we don't look forward to our own judgment, but there is nothing we like better than judging others. It is a national pastime. We love to score points and settle accounts, talk behind people's backs.

Jesus says this: 'The measure you give to others will be the measure you will get back. Pay attention to the log in your eye rather than taking such pleasure in pointing out the speck that is in your brother's!'

Oh, what a different world it would be if we could take off the judge's wig and stop passing sentence on each other with such monstrous regularity! What irony there is in what we do—we all sit together in the same rocky boat of human failure, awaiting the judgment of God.

The season of Advent begins tomorrow. Traditionally, Advent is seen as a time to consider judgment. It is therefore quite a relief to remember that judgment belongs to God, not us. The judge that God has appointed is Jesus—one we know is merciful and hates evil, but is infinitely kind. Because he is one of us—one who knows the temptations that ensnare us—we can approach God without fear. So, from the challenges of Christian faith we next turn to the consolations.

### Prayer

*Merciful God, soften my heart. When I am tempted to judge others, fill me with remorse for my own failings. When I stand before your throne of judgment, give me the humility to receive the grace you offer me in Christ.*

*SC*

### Matthew 10:29–31 (NRSV)

# The affirmation of love

[Jesus said] 'Are not two sparrows sold for a penny? Yet not one of them will fall to the ground unperceived by your Father. And even the hairs of your head are all counted. So do not be afraid; you are of more value than many sparrows.'

Most of us are looking for love in our lives in one way or another. We search it out, we crave it. Yet, at the same time, we find it hard to love ourselves, harder to love others and virtually impossible to love God! It is funny being so bad at something that we want so much. Who will teach us how to love?

Today is the first Sunday of Advent. It is the beginning of that season of the Christian year when we look forward to the birth of Christ and think, too, about meeting God face to face. For, while we are looking for love, God, who is the source of love, is looking for us. In the Christ child, God comes to find us. That's what the word 'Advent' means—coming. God is coming to show us what love is like.

The Advent of God is glorious—the fullness of God in a tiny, helpless child. The Advent of God is ambiguous—there is no sure-fire way of knowing that this astonishing story is true. Indeed, many will meet this man and never know who he is. Many will hear about him today and dismiss his claims.

We, though, have caught a glimpse of who Christ is. We see in Christ the searching love of God. We receive from Christ the invitation to share God's life. That is the great consolation of the Christian faith: God loves us with the intimacy of a lover. God delights in us. God longs for us to be part of a community of love that is the community of God. He counts the freckles on our faces and the hairs on our heads.

In the Christ who is coming, God offers this invitation to know and be known and discover love. God wants what we most deeply want. God alone can provide it.

### Prayer

*Generous God, thank you for the love you give us in Christ.*
*Replenish our hearts and help us to love in return.*

*SC*

# The God who reaches out to us

[Jesus said] 'Then the righteous will answer him [the Son of Man], "Lord, when was it that we saw you hungry and gave you food, or thirsty and gave you something to drink? And when was it that we saw you a stranger and welcomed you, or naked and gave you clothing? And when was it that we saw you sick or in prison and visited you?" And the king will answer them, "Truly I tell you, just as you did it to one of the least of these who are members of my family, you did it to me."'

As we saw in last Monday's and Tuesday's readings, loving our enemies is horribly difficult. Most of us will fail, but there is some solace to be found from knowing that, whenever we minister to someone in need, whoever they are and however unlovable they may appear, we are ministering to Jesus. That is the comforting and challenging message of the last of three great parables of judgment that Jesus delivers in Matthew's Gospel, just days before his death. Jesus will be present to us in all those who suffer. We will minister to him when we minister to those in need. We will not necessarily recognize him, which won't necessarily matter. What does matter is that we reach out to those who are hungry and helpless. Furthermore, following Jesus and living his way might also mean that we end up hungry, naked and imprisoned ourselves. Then as others minister to us, so they will serve Christ.

At the very least, reaching out to the hungry should mean reaching out to *all* the hungry, not just the ones we think deserve our care.

In the midst of the challenge of doing this, let us also rejoice at the consolation it offers. We are not going to be judged by what we know. We are not going to be judged by the firmness of our beliefs, the strictness of our morals or our adherence to a particular religious brand. In the end, we will be with him because of what Jesus has done in reaching out to us, his hungry and thirsty little ones, and the ways in which we have reached out to others, whether we saw Christ in them or not.

### Prayer

*Compassionate God, whether we recognize you or not, shape our lives for service.*

SC

# Peace the world cannot give

[Jesus said] 'I have said these things to you while I am still with you. But the Advocate, the Holy Spirit, whom the Father will send in my name, will teach you everything, and remind you of all that I have said to you. Peace I leave with you; my peace I give to you. I do not give to you as the world gives. Do not let your hearts be troubled, and do not let them be afraid.'

Christian peace is not the silence after the guns have finished firing. Christian peace—the peace that Jesus gives—is reconciliation painfully embraced. God's peace gathers together the shattered fragments of our lives and builds them into a new creation.

It is a peace that is a gift of God's Holy Spirit. It constantly leads us to Jesus and truth. In John's Gospel the Spirit is called the 'Paraclete'. It is a Greek word that is hard to translate into English. Sometimes a legal word such as 'advocate' is used (as in this translation), but a counselling term such as 'comforter' or 'consoler' would also be correct.

In Advent, God comes to us in Christ and prepares us afresh for the joy and completeness of heaven. Meanwhile, what passes for peace in the world is often no more than an empty truce, a stand-off. We hide behind barriers of separation, like the wall that still stands in the centre of Belfast, like the wall around Bethlehem itself, like the gated communities that have emerged in our fearful and affluent suburbs.

The peace of Christ is, first, an inner assurance—a consolation—that we are loved, the ultimate victory is already secure, nothing can confound us. Then it spreads. That consolation brings freedom—freedom to dismantle barriers, build friendships, love enemies, turn the other cheek. It is peace like an overflowing stream that gushes from the heart of Christ to the heart of each believer. It irrigates the soul. It changes the world. It leads us to speak up for God's justice.

### Prayer

*Reconciling God, break down the barriers of separation that keep us from you and each other. Unclench our fists and, where backs are turned in resentful acquiescence, turn us round to encounter and embrace. Give us the peace of Christ and stir our souls that we may make peace in the world.*

SC

# The God who washes our feet

Now before the festival of the Passover, Jesus knew that his hour had come to depart from this world and go to the Father. Having loved his own who were in the world, he loved them to the end... And during supper Jesus, knowing that the Father had given all things into his hands, and that he had come from God and was going to God, got up from the table, took off his outer robe, and tied a towel around himself. Then he poured water into a basin and began to wash the disciples' feet and to wipe them with the towel that was tied around him.

The challenge to be a servant in the Christian life is met and sustained by the astonishing example of Jesus' own servant heart. There are numerous examples of this in the Gospels, but they reach their climax in this amazing episode the night before he died. Knowing what was in the mind of his betrayer and guessing which of his disciples would fall away, and just before he broke bread with them, Jesus took off his outer robes, tied a towel round his waist and washed their feet.

This in itself was not such an unusual custom. It was commonplace in the Middle East of Jesus' day for a servant to perform such a menial but welcome task. What is unusual here is that it is Jesus himself who does this for his friends. It seems the wrong way round. So much so, that, as the story continues, Peter recoils from receiving this service from Jesus (vv. 6–8).

Jesus perseveres: 'Unless I wash you, you have no share with me,' he says.

Again, we find challenge and consolation bound together in these verses. We are called to be servants. That is challenging enough in itself, but we are also called to allow Jesus to serve us. Sometimes *receiving* service is harder than *giving* it. We have to relinquish power. Once we do let go and once we allow Jesus to wash us, then a wave of relief and joy and consolation flows through us. We have a share in him.

**Prayer**

*Steadfast, servant God, thank you for serving me in Christ. Save me from the pride that would refuse the love of others. Console me with the living waters, Christ himself.*

*SC*

MARK 2:3–9 (NRSV)

# The assurance of sins forgiven

Then some people came, bringing to him [Jesus] a paralysed man, carried by four of them. And when they could not bring him to Jesus because of the crowd, they removed the roof above him; and... they let down the mat on which the paralytic lay. When Jesus saw their faith, he said to the paralytic, 'Son, your sins are forgiven.' Now some of the scribes were sitting there, questioning in their hearts, 'Why does this fellow speak in this way? It is blasphemy! Who can forgive sins but God alone?'... [Jesus] said to them, '... Which is easier, to say to the paralytic, "Your sins are forgiven", or to say, "Stand up and take your mat and walk"?'

What greater words of hope and consolation could there be than those? Your sins are forgiven: get up, be free. Once again, however, the consolation also contains the sting of challenge.

The men on the roof haven't brought their friend to be forgiven, they want Jesus to heal him. At first, though, Jesus doesn't seem to notice the man's physical disability. He looks deeper. He reaches to the heart. He notices what we need most.

We all have our ailments and discomforts and so much to lower through the roof for God's attention, but, when God looks at us, when God beholds us lying, vulnerable, before him, he ministers to our deepest need. In this man's case it was his sin. Can it be very different for us? It is the vanity of our many sinful, wrong choices that most debilitates us and, on that last day, when we do meet God face to face, nothing else will matter—we will know the mercy of God and feel his everlasting arms around us.

In this story, Jesus heals the man's paralysis when his authority to forgive sins is questioned, but that is also a sign of God ministering to the whole person. Even though we all face suffering of different kinds and must one day face death, God's forgiveness and healing are the ultimate promise of the Christian faith.

### Prayer

*Merciful God, meet me at the point of my deepest need; heal and forgive me through Jesus.*

*SC*

ROMANS 8:18–21, 26 (NRSV)

# The Spirit who prays in us

I consider that the sufferings of this present time are not worth comparing with the glory about to be revealed to us. For the creation waits with eager longing for the revealing of the children of God; for the creation was subjected to futility, not of its own will but by the will of the one who subjected it, in hope that the creation itself will be set free from its bondage to decay and will obtain the freedom of the glory of the children of God… Likewise the Spirit helps us in our weakness; for we do not know how to pray as we ought, but that very Spirit intercedes with sighs too deep for words.

If the Bible were a mountain range, then surely Romans chapter 8 would be the peak! Paul presents a vision of the whole of creation longing to be set free and have its true glory restored and revealed. Not only the creation, says Paul, but us as well. The Spirit of God wants to bring us to adoption into a new family. That same Spirit, who is called the comforter, the consoler, will help us in our weakness and pray within us.

Finding the desire to pray and accept the free gift of what God has done for us in Christ can seem hard. That discipline, which enables the whole of our life to be aligned with and shaped by God's will, seems harder still, but there is more good news. Even prayer is not something we do on our own. The Holy Spirit prays within us with sighs too deep for words, enabling us to know God. 'Because you are his children,' says

Paul, 'God has sent the Spirit of his Son into our hearts, crying, "Abba! Father!" So you are no longer a slave but a child, and if a child then also an heir, through God' (Galatians:4:6–7).

It is all a gift! At the times of greatest testing and challenge, the Holy Spirit will speak in and through you (see Matthew 10:20). 'You did not choose me,' says Jesus, 'but I chose you' (John 15:16). Everything that God has done in Christ is for us.

### Prayer

*Generous God, give me the consolation of your Spirit and pray within me, aligning my heart and will to Christ.*

*SC*

LUKE 23:39–43 (NRSV)

# The scandalous hospitality of God

One of the criminals who were hanged there kept deriding him and saying, 'Are you not the Messiah? Save yourself and us!' But the other rebuked him, saying, 'Do you not fear God, since you are under the same sentence of condemnation? And we indeed have been condemned justly, for we are getting what we deserve for our deeds, but this man has done nothing wrong.' Then he said, 'Jesus, remember me when you come into your kingdom.' He replied, 'Truly I tell you, today you will be with me in Paradise.'

This fortunate fellow is usually referred to as the penitent thief, but is penitence the best way to think about his attitude? He rebukes his fellow criminal for haranguing Jesus as they are both getting what they deserve, but that is realism, not repentance, surely. Perhaps we should call him the realistic thief. Then, he acknowledges that Jesus has done nothing wrong. Perhaps we should call him the magnanimous thief. Then (maybe he's heard of Jesus and his teaching about God's kingdom) he turns to him saying, 'Remember me in that kingdom of yours.' Perhaps we should call him the optimistic thief.

The point of the story, however—the final upside-down, winning trump of grace that confounds all the legalistic point-scoring of the religious and the powerful—is that this is all it takes. Here is the optimistic thief in the last chance saloon of life, not so much penitent as hopeful, reaching out to this dying man he has vaguely heard of and whose merciful generosity he has witnessed, saying, 'Remember me', and that is sufficient. Jesus reaches back and tells him, 'Today paradise is yours.'

Perhaps we persist in labelling this man penitent because we can't cope with the scandal of a gospel that really is free. We want to put some preconditions in place. The consolation of the gospel is that the optimistic undeserving are as welcome as everyone else in the kingdom of heaven. The challenge is to live our lives with the same profligate love.

### Prayer

*Loving God, while we were still sinners, Jesus died for us. Welcome us, and all who turn to you in hope, into the slap-up supper of heaven where every slate is wiped clean and every tear wiped away.*

SC

# The proverbs of Solomon: Proverbs 10—16

I suppose most people assume, as I did, that the book of Proverbs was written entirely by King Solomon—famous for being the wisest character in the Old Testament. In fact, it appears that there are three authors or collectors—one being Solomon, the other two being Agur and Lemuel. Of course, Solomon is by far the best-known of this trio. He was the son of David and seems to have inherited his father's interest in and love for words.

Proverbs is a collection of wise sayings, many of which emphasize the contrast between the path of righteousness and the path of evil and laziness. The consequences of following either of these paths are clearly stated and there is little attempt to analyse or examine the reasons for people finding themselves on such starkly different routes. There are certainly gems to be found in this famous book of the Bible, but they do tend to be hidden in the long grass of acres of admonishment and advice, much of which appears to make the same point over and over again, but in slightly different ways.

The section I am looking at in these notes covers chapters 10 to 16, which, as far as I know, are believed to be the work of Solomon. I have tried to arrange verses in groups that reflect a particular theme or idea. Inevitably, some of these themes tend to overlap, but I hope the approach in each case is a clear and individual one.

At the centre of all the wisdom expressed in these verses is 'fear of the Lord'—an attitude that implies reliance on God and a deep respect for his majesty. Good old Solomon may have been a bit repetitive, but he was anxious to convey his belief that God is our creator and therefore knows exactly what is best for us. As usual, this Old Testament teaching is best seen as a signpost to Jesus. The light that it conveys would be seen in its purity and completeness when he came to earth.

Writing these notes has been an interesting journey for me. At times I have found the repetition quite irksome and, being used to seeing all 59 sides of every issue, I have found the black and white nature of Solomon's arguments quite difficult to handle. However, that's my problem. Come with me and see what you think.

*Adrian Plass*

# Watch your mouth!

Whoever winks maliciously causes grief, and a chattering fool comes to ruin. The mouth of the righteous is a fountain of life, but violence overwhelms the mouth of the wicked... The one who conceals hatred has lying lips, and whoever spreads slander is a fool. When words are many, sin is not absent, but the wise hold their tongues. The tongue of the righteous is choice silver, but the heart of the wicked is of little value. The lips of the righteous nourish many, but fools die for lack of judgment.

Over the last couple of decades, I have written more than 25 books and spoken to hundreds of thousands of people. I say this not to impress (although I secretly hope you will be a little bit impressed, of course), but because I fear that I may qualify as a 'chattering fool'. I have said so much to so many people about so many things, and now here is Solomon saying that sin is not absent when words are many and ruin awaits those who babble foolishly on without regard for their listeners.

In this connection we might observe a broad gap in today's Church between the teachings of Jesus and the ways in which some of us actually behave. Prayer is an example. In Matthew 6:7, Jesus says, 'And when you pray, do not keep on babbling like pagans, for they think they will be heard because of their many words.'

Bewitchingly sane, isn't it? One can only assume that those who produce eternal, swelling crescendos of prayer or 'marinade' long-suffering listeners in endless, meandering rivers of earnest exhortation have never actually read the Gospels. The principle we all need to learn seems to be that a few well-chosen and sincere words can work wonders and might even offer a fountain of life to those who are thirsty.

I am a little cheered by realizing that, on one level, I do have less to say about my faith nowadays. There was an aura of hideous certainty about my pronouncements at one time—lots of chatter, but limited substance. Now I know that I am greatly blessed and deeply troubled and that fact can be expressed in a very few words. Having said that, here I am using lots of words to tell you about it! Oh, well...

### Prayer

*Hush my mouth, Lord.*

AP

# Words of wisdom

The proverbs of Solomon: Wise children bring joy to their fathers, but the foolish bring grief to their mothers... The wise in heart accept commands, but a chattering fool comes to ruin... Wisdom is found on the lips of the discerning, but a rod is for the back of one who lacks judgment. The wise store up knowledge, but the mouth of a fool invites ruin... Fools find pleasure in evil conduct, but those who have insight delight in wisdom... The mouth of the righteous brings forth wisdom, but a perverse tongue will be cut out.

These verses are about the benefits of wisdom and the consequences of foolishness. The chattering fool (remember him, or her, from yesterday?) once more courts ruin, those who lack judgment make a rod for their backs and perverse tongues will be cut out.

Strong stuff. Though I cannot dispute that wisdom is preferable to foolishness, it seems a bit much that Solomon of all people has so much to say on the subject. Famously wise and knowledgeable, we learn in 1 Kings that he ended his career as ruler of Israel by turning to the gods of his foreign wives and actually building temples to Chemosh and Molech, detestable gods of Moab and the Ammonites. This enraged God and resulted in disaster for Solomon's son Rehoboam.

Two questions. How could Solomon the wise be so incredibly stupid? Well, sex and flattery were probably as seductive then as they are now. They say that there is no

fool like an old fool and they are probably right in this case.

The second question is trickier. If Solomon could mess up so badly, what hope is there for us in our feeble-witted attempts to get things right? My prayers for wisdom in this matter have been unsuccessful, but I have a suggestion. Solomon's knowledge and wisdom would have told him quite clearly that his disobedience and betrayal of God was utter madness.

We know a few things, don't we? We are not Solomons, but we can aim to live and operate and remain faithful within the limited boundaries of the wisdom we have been given. That will use up most of our time and effort and I suspect that, as far as God is concerned, it will be enough.

## Reflection

*Don't be wise after the event.*
*It doesn't work.*

AP

PROVERBS 11:16–17, 24–26 (NIV)

# Kindness and generosity

A kind-hearted woman gains respect, but ruthless men gain only wealth. Those who are kind benefit only themselves, but the cruel bring trouble on themselves... One gives freely, yet gains even more; another withholds unduly, but comes to poverty. A generous person will prosper; the one who refreshes others will be refreshed. People curse those who hoard grain, but blessing crowns those who are willing to sell.

G.K. Chesterton talks about a Scotsman who gave away millions in order to hide the fact that he was mean. This bizarre ploy may have deceived those who never actually met the gentleman in question, but I doubt if he would have been able to fake the kind of inner generosity that is visible through the windows of the soul.

I love genuine kindness, don't you? I have a friend who exists on a very limited income, but somehow gives the impression of having access to great wealth. I think it has something to do with the light hold he has on his own possessions and the open-handedness with which he shares whatever is surplus to his basic requirements. Solomon says that a kind-hearted woman earns respect and I am pretty sure that the same is true of my friend. He has certainly gained my respect and I would love others to see me in the same light, but here is the difficult question. Do I, in any practical sense, actually want to be like him?

It occurs to me that an honest reply to that question is reflected in my attitude to dieting. I would be more than happy to keep to a regular diet as long as there was no question of reducing the amount of food I ate. This dismal equation tends to reproduce itself in all sorts of areas in my life.

I guess that it comes down to a question of belief. Solomon says that a generous man will prosper. Jesus says the same. Store up treasure in heaven (Matthew 6:20) and spend it when you get there. I have to ask myself if I really do believe that ultimate spiritual prosperity is as real and assured as worldly wealth. Sometimes. Occasionally. Yes and no. Difficult, isn't it?

### Prayer

*Warm my heart, Lord. Help me to practise being kind and generous. I want it to be deep and real.*

AP

PROVERBS 11:5, 8, 19, 21, 27–28 (NIV)

# The fruits of righteousness

The righteousness of the blameless makes a straight way for them, but the wicked are brought down by their own wickedness... The righteous are rescued from trouble, and it comes on the wicked instead... The truly righteous attain life, but those who pursue evil go to their death... Be sure of this: the wicked will not go unpunished, but those who are righteous will go free... Whoever seeks good finds goodwill, but evil comes to the one who searches for it. Those who trust in their riches will fall, but the righteous will thrive like a green leaf.

I don't suppose Solomon's scribe was allowed any comment on the prolific outpourings of his master, otherwise he might have expressed scepticism about the contents of these verses. If Job had been there he might have had something to say as well, but we'll return to him in a moment because he had the advantage of seeing both sides of the righteousness coin.

'The thing is,' our cheeky scribe might declare, 'these things are just not true, are they, your Majesty? Righteous men aren't always rescued from trouble and the wicked aren't always brought down by their wickedness. Well, they aren't, are they? As for being poor but righteous and thriving like a green leaf, it sounds very nice, but lots of them end up not thriving at all. And,' he might well continue, warming to his theme, 'I've tried seeking good and, I have to say, I've had very mixed results. I'd leave this last lot out— what do you think?'

Job might have saved the scribe from summary decapitation by pointing out, too, that the heart of righteousness does not lie in cold, mechanical acts of virtue or restraint, but in a developing relationship with the God whose power over the destiny of men and women stretches far beyond the bounds of time and space.

Good people are not always rewarded in this life and, equally, evildoers often evade punishment for the period of their lifetime. Thousands of years after the reign of Solomon, however, the face of Stephen was seen to shine like an angel as the crowds stoned him to death. Why? Because he knew that the best was yet to come and the best would be a million times better than any temporal satisfaction.

### Prayer

*Lord, teach us to be good for the right reasons.*

AP

Proverbs 12:3, 7–8, 13, 21, 24, 26 (NIV)

# Choosing the road

No one can be established through wickedness, but the righteous cannot be uprooted... The wicked are overthrown and are no more, but the house of the righteous stands firm. One is praised according to one's wisdom, but people with warped minds are despised... Evildoers are trapped by their sinful talk, but the righteous escape trouble... No harm befalls the righteous, but the wicked have their fill of trouble... Diligent hands will rule, but laziness ends in slave labour... The righteous are cautious in friendship, but the way of the wicked leads them astray.

Why do the wicked appear so attractive sometimes? In every generation there are parents who find it necessary to peel or crowbar their growing children away from 'undesirable' characters who have stirred the imagination of impressionable minds. Solomon says that men with warped minds are despised, but I know from my own experience that there can be an enlivening and creative aspect to contact with those who actively court the darkness.

Before you run away with the idea that I spend my days with the local coven, I should make it clear that I am talking about men and women who are as willing to dive into the dark sides of their lives as into the light. I have made my own excursions into the shadows and I have no wish to go there again, not least because I agree with Solomon when he says that, ultimately, the way of the wicked leads them astray. That said, I do understand the fascination with night.

I think God does as well. The roots of great good and great evil are the same in the lives of many human beings. One example is King David—a man after God's own heart with a personality that was capable of extravagant goodness and equally extravagant, morally abandoned evil. Perhaps one thing that God loved about David was that very tendency to plunge his head and heart so totally into everything that he did, good or bad.

The trick, of course, is in steering and selection. The American poet Robert Frost famously talks of two roads that diverged in a wood. He ends the poem by saying that his choice of the road less travelled has made all the difference. Choice is everything.

**Prayer**
*Lead us to the light, Lord.*

*AP*

# Don't be stupid

Whoever loves discipline loves knowledge, but whoever hates correction is stupid... Those who work their land will have abundant food, but those who chase fantasies lack judgment... The way of fools seems right to them, but the wise listen to advice. Fools show their annoyance at once, but the prudent overlook an insult... The prudent keep their knowledge to themselves, but the heart of fools blurts out folly.

You know, I could get bored with Solomon. Talk about saying the same thing 93 times in slightly different ways. Talk about seeing the world like an early Charlie Chaplin film, in stark black and white. Talk about stating the blindingly obvious. 'It's not a good idea to be stupid.' That's the message of these verses, and, of course, it's a completely different message from the one that says it's better to be wise—not.

Mind you, times have changed, I suppose. In Solomon's day, a person who chased fantasies probably did end up with no food. Nowadays, she is just as likely to write bestselling children's books that sell by the bucketload, are turned into blockbuster films and earn her millions. Similarly, there are good career opportunities for those who blurt out folly, for instance, in popular art criticism, not to mention politics.

Yes, I am being flippant, but there is a genuine question behind my irritation. What if I am stupid?

What if that's the way I'm made? Is it really possible to change by an act of the will into someone very sensible? Solomon seems to view it that way and, of course, I can make a few decisions that might help, but I don't think I'm going to put much of a dent in my obtuseness, do you? What on earth are we stupid ones to do?

Two responses suggest themselves. First of all, we don't live in the Old Testament. We are friends and disciples of Jesus. Second, following on from that point, whenever I ask a question like this, there is a passage from the book of Romans (7:24–25) that flies unbidden into my mind: 'What a wretched man I am! Who will rescue me from this body of death? Thanks be to God—through Jesus Christ our Lord!'

### Reflection

*Whatever the problem, take it to Jesus. He is our refuge. Let it all out.*

*AP*

# Tough love

A wise child heeds a parent's instruction, but a mocker does not listen to rebuke… Whoever scorns instruction will pay for it, but whoever respects a command is rewarded. The teaching of the wise is a fountain of life, turning people from the snares of death… Whoever walks with the wise grows wise, but a companion of fools suffers harm.

They say that you only become better at tennis by playing people more skilful than yourself. Of course, you can confine yourself to opponents you are certain to beat, but you have to be a certain kind of person to gain satisfaction from such predictable victories. In these verses Solomon is making a similar point about the development of character and moral strength. If you wish to grow and move forward as a human being, you have to accept your deficiencies and seek change by taking discipline and instruction from those who are wiser than you. As usual, though, the process is not as simple as it sounds. First of all, some of us are blind to our faults.

I met a man just the other day whose wife had left him. It was the third long-term relationship of his life and, in each case, the ladies concerned had decided, for one reason or another, that they had had enough of him. After listening to a long list of criticisms directed at all three of his ex-partners, I asked him if he felt that he had contributed in any way to these break-ups. His reply flabbergasted me: 'No,' he said after considering calmly for a moment, 'I can't recall ever doing anything wrong at all.' 'What, nothing?' I said. 'No, nothing I can remember. It was always them who spoiled it,' he said. What can you say?

The second kind of complication involves those people (and I have been one myself) whose sense of self is so tentative and poorly constructed that they are terrified of allowing any criticism or constructive advice to disturb the fragility of the personality they have settled for. Occasionally a little deconstruction is necessary before something can be built, but it is so frightening.

Denial and fear: two common obstacles to learning from others. Do you want to improve your tennis?

### Prayer

*Father, some of us dread change in ourselves. Help us to be brave.*

AP

Proverbs 13:4, 8, 11–12, 19, 25 (NIV)

# Satisfaction

The sluggard craves and gets nothing, but the desires of the diligent are fully satisfied... The rich may ransom their lives, but the poor hear no threats... Dishonest money dwindles away, but whoever gathers money little by little makes it grow. Hope deferred makes the heart sick, but a longing fulfilled is a tree of life... A longing fulfilled is sweet to the soul, but fools detest turning from evil... The righteous eat to their hearts' content, but the stomach of the wicked goes hungry.

Solomon is talking about the route to genuine satisfaction or fulfilment. His arguments are predictable. The sluggard gets nothing, dishonest money does you no good, sinners run out of luck and the wicked go hungry. Good, hardworking people, we are not surprised to learn, eat well and are satisfied. All quite right and proper, of course, but the only bit that really moves me is the first half of verse 19: 'A longing fulfilled is sweet to the soul.' So it is, but what might that mean?

Yesterday evening, my wife and I put our border collie in the back of the car and drove down to the village of East Dean to have a drink at the Tiger Inn. It was a wonderful early autumn evening, the whole world was bathed in a rich, orangey-red light that settled and intensified as darkness pressed it to the land. Driving through Jevington and on between voluptuous, swaying fields towards Friston was a poem of light and texture. Arriving in East Dean, we threw a ball for Lucy on the green before ordering drinks and crisps and settling down at one of the tables outside the pub. Bridget had her hair cut particularly well yesterday. She looked relaxed and attractive. I was as scruffy as ever. That little island of time was exquisite. We loved and relished and valued it. Being there, being together and being happy was probably about as fulfilling as it gets. That's how I felt. It was certainly sweet to the soul. Would Solomon have agreed with me if he had joined us at the pub for a small port and a packet of ready salted? All the stuff he talks about is bound up in there somewhere, so I think that he probably would. What do you think?

### Reflection

*Thanks for the sweet, fulfilling times.*

AP

# Secrets of the heart

The person whose walk is upright fears the Lord, but the one whose ways are devious despises him... A truthful witness does not deceive, but a false witness pours out lies... Each heart knows its own bitterness, and no one else can share its joy... There is a way that seems right to a person, but in the end it leads to darth. Even in laughter the heart may ache, and joy may end in grief... The simple believe anything, but the prudent give thought to their steps... A truthful witness saves lives, but a false witness is deceitful.

Truth is one of those words that Christians use a lot. It's so short, so easy to say and sometimes quite easy to understand. Verse 25, for instance, suggests that witnesses should tell the truth, especially if someone's life is at stake. No arguing with that, is there? We might crumple under tough questioning and end up a bit confused, but we would want to be honest and get it right. Verse 10 is much more intriguing and a whole lot less accessible to simple argument. It is about the secrets of the heart. Each heart, says Solomon, 'knows its own bitterness'.

Do you agree with him? Does each of us conceal a little burning well of resentment, something from the past that hurt us and is unlikely ever to be resolved? I have just stopped to ask myself the same question. My first answer was firmly in the negative, but, then, as I allowed my memory to explore the past, I began to realize that there are some fires that still burn inside me, some of them very small, but definitely not extinguished. How about you?

In the second half of the verse, Solomon claims that no one else can share the joy that is in the heart of the individual. I don't know if I agree with that or not. My experience is that people are far less able to conceal joy than grief—it kind of spills out of them. Having said that, there is a species of joy—for me a sort of cosmic dimension of gratitude—that is not explainable and not always appropriate to share, especially when others are going through bad times.

So, there is bitterness and joy in our hearts. God is the only one who really understands.

### Prayer

*Search our hearts, Lord. Tell us if anything needs to be done.*

*AP*

PROVERBS 14:1, 3, 6, 8, 22–23 (NIV)

# Cut off your nose to spite your face?

The wise woman builds her house, but with her own hands the foolish one tears hers down... The talk of fools brings a rod to their backs, but the lips of the wise protect them... The mocker seeks wisdom and finds none, but knowledge comes easily to the discerning... The wisdom of the prudent is to give thought to their ways, but the folly of fools is deception... Do not those who plot evil go astray? But those who plan what is good find love and faithfulness. All hard work brings a profit, but mere talk leads only to poverty.

I have always had a soft spot for people who are self-destructive. I saw a lot of this kind of behaviour during the years when I was working with children in care. Sometimes it was caused by the pressure of imminent success. A boy or girl might have been on the very edge of acquiring all the things that they had lacked and longed for throughout their deprived lives. Suddenly the terrible fear of failure, the dread of letting themselves down in a new and unfamiliar environment, would so overwhelm them that they would deliberately engineer the destruction of their dreams. It was terrible and sad and I hate to recall it.

In these verses, Solomon is clearly not interested in any attempt to analyse the reasons for a foolish woman tearing down her own house. She is simply observed to be foolish rather than wise and foolishness is a fault, not an affliction. Similarly, the mocker, the evil plotter and the mere talker receive their just deserts and will definitely not be sent off for a course of counselling designed to ensure a change of heart and eventual moral rehabilitation.

I know that we live in a very different age, one in which we are no longer sure what is meant by personal responsibility, which does trouble me. We can make choices and sometimes have to pay for what we choose. The fact is, though, that if the people who have loved me and the God whom I try to serve had not understood and overlooked my destructive and self-destructive behaviour in the past, I would be little more than a remnant now. Thank you to all of them.

### Prayer

*Help us to be patient and understanding with ourselves and each other, Lord.*

AP

# Spread a little tenderness

A gentle answer turns away wrath, but a harsh word stirs up anger... The tongue that brings healing is a tree of life, but a deceitful tongue crushes the spirit... A happy heart makes the face cheerful, but heartache crushes the spirit... A person finds joy in giving an apt reply—and how good is a timely word!... A cheerful look brings joy to the heart, and good news gives health to the bones.

I have described elsewhere the ridiculous fantasy I once entertained concerning three different postmen who brought letters to our door. My fantasy, quite simply, was that each brought a different kind of post. The avuncular, older gentleman brought letters from old friends and unexpected cheques. The young man who sometimes filled in for him was only able to manage circulars and leaflets, while the rather severe third person, who happened to belong to a grindingly spontaneous church at the other end of town, specialized in bills and dismal communications from the bank.

All nonsense, of course, but that's how it seemed and, in a sense, that's how it can seem with people in general. I suppose it's something to do with one's view of the world. I know a lady, for instance, who consistently lives out the final proverb in the list above. Full of apt replies and timely words, she always has a cheerful attitude, despite chronic illness, and the good news of her presence really does 'give health to my bones'. I am refreshed by her positive approach to life. By contrast, I know a fellow who appears to live in a different universe. Trust nobody. Nothing is as it seems. Smiles and encouragement are in short supply and should be given away rarely, if ever. Far from turning away wrath with a gentle answer, he is more likely to meet a gentle question with a blast of wrath. Strange and sad, isn't it, that two people living in the same world should see it so differently? One brings treasure and finds it. The other expects the worst and almost invariably gets it.

By the way, I recently tried meeting wrath with a gentle answer even though I didn't feel like it, and it really did work like magic. Give it a go.

## Prayer

*Give us a healing tongue, Lord. We want to be helpful.*

AP

# The roots of happiness

Better a little with the fear of the Lord than great wealth with turmoil. Better a meal of vegetables where there is love than a fattened calf with hatred.

I suppose these two verses are not saying anything substantially different from the ones we have already read, but they do offer something very important about the establishment of priorities.

Priorities change over the years. Certainly, in my own case there has been a movement towards much simpler things. I have been trying to think through the areas that are most important to me. Indulge me in a little whim for a moment. Suppose Jesus were to appear in the flesh, sitting in the chair just over there on the other side of my computer. 'Adrian,' he says, 'I can give you three things on the spot—anything you want. What's it going to be?'

I think carefully, swiftly dismissing a series of trivial indulgences that spring to mind. Three things. Don't get it wrong. 'Peace is the first thing. Peace with you, peace with myself. Peace with what has been and peace with what is to come. That's not three things, is it?' He reassures me that it's not. 'Right, well, the second one is about my family. I'd like them all to love you and love each other and love me and come and have meals with us and be happy. That must be four things, though, isn't it?' Apparently not. 'Well, I suppose the third thing would be to help others to find the first two things—if that's possible.'

He nods, makes a note on a sheet of paper and passes it to an angel standing at his shoulder. Is that a good sign? I hope so.

Yes, those are definitely the things I want most in my life. I agree with Solomon, I would rather have those things and live on vegetables than feast on the fatted calf and mourn the loss of those I love. I would also much rather live on very little and be at peace with God than wallow in great wealth and be constantly aware that my soul is filled with darkness.

### Reflection

*These things are the roots,*
*the foliage and the bloom*
*of true happiness.*

*AP*

PROVERBS 16:5, 18–19, 31 (NIV)

# Humility

The Lord detests all the proud of heart. Be sure of this: they will not go unpunished... Pride goes before destruction, a haughty spirit before a fall. Better to be lowly in spirit and among the oppressed than to share plunder with the proud... Grey hair is a crown of splendour; it is attained by a righteous life.

Ah, something I know about. Humility is definitely one of my strengths, I'm proud to say. Seriously, though, true humility is so beautiful. Verse 19 reminds me of Lily, an elderly lady who used to be in our house group and is now away dancing in heaven. Lily worked as a missionary nurse in Africa for most of her life. Genuinely lowly in spirit, she was totally committed to people who were beaten down in every sense. She would never have wanted to be anywhere else or serve in any other way. Lily made me feel good, probably because she assumed that I loved God with the simplicity and devotion that characterized her own walk with Jesus. Don't you love people like that? They place the mantle of their heavenly Father on everyone they meet, making them feel a little bit better about themselves. What a gift to the rest of us.

Humility can't be faked or manufactured and, of course, if we ever achieve it we shall be too humble to realize it. So, I guess we'll just have to keep praying, do our best and leave God to sort the rest out.

Incidentally, according to verse 31, I have definitely been living a righteous life. Unfortunately, my wife has just pointed out that in Solomon's day old age and its accompanying grey hair would have been much rarer and almost certainly a sign that the person in question had lived, at the very least, a moderate, well-ordered life. My father-in-law, who took moderation to wild extremes and lived to be 96, had a fine head of grey hair and was remarkably fit until the last couple of years of his life.

As for me, well, I certainly am doing well on the greying front, but there is still a bit of an ongoing problem with the humility.

**Prayer**

*Lord, thank you so much for people like Lily. Teach us humility.*

*AP*

# Who's steering?

To human beings belong the plans of the heart, but from the Lord comes the reply of the tongue… Commit to the Lord whatever you do, and your plans will succeed… In your heart you may plan your course, but the Lord determines your steps… Honest scales and balances are from the Lord; all the weights in the bag are of his making… The lot is cast into the lap, but its every decision is from the Lord.

Verse 9 reminds me of a comment by the American writer Anne Lamott. Sometimes, she says, parents buy toy driving systems for their very small children so that they can sit in the back of the car turning their plastic steering wheels, pretending that they are actually driving the vehicle. Every now and then, the adult driver glances at his or her small charge in the mirror, smiling at the earnestness with which the child concentrates on the task. Perhaps, says Anne Lamott, God manages our lives in a similar way. We kid ourselves that steering is our responsibility, tackling the job with grim determination. Meanwhile, God, who is actually directing the course of our destiny, looks round with a smile from time to time, amused by our deluded assumption that we know where to go and what to do.

Like all charmingly tidy metaphors, this one has its limits. We are not absolved of responsibility for controlling our lives. Every day involves choices and any one of them might have a significant impact on the future. If, however, we really believe that God is in a fatherly relationship with us and his power is as potent as his love, then, as Solomon is saying in this collection of proverbs, we are right to assume he will never let anything hurt the most vulnerable area of our being.

Problems arise, of course, when we fail to agree with God on the nature of that area. Can parents who have suffered the devastating loss of a child, for instance, believe that God really does have a grip on their lives? Such things are hard, but how are we to survive tragedies like bereavement if we lose sight of the fact that, night and day, and in the most important sense of all, his hand really is on the wheel?

**Prayer**

*Deepen our faith, Lord.*

AP

# Christmas words

It's that time of year again when we focus our attention on the birth of Jesus and celebrate together the wonder of the incarnation. Whatever you think of the Christmas season as such, it provides us with a natural opportunity to revisit the familiar, yet amazing, story of the coming of the Saviour and reflect once more on one of the great mysteries of our faith—how it is that God could become a human being.

As we read some of the well-loved passages from Luke and John, we will focus on some of the key words of Christmas: child, joy, angels, light and so on. Can I suggest that, as we do this, you also try to keep in mind the bigger picture of what is taking place. Remember, for example, that a divine plan and purpose is being worked out here, a plan that started way back in the book of Genesis when the first promise of a Saviour was made ('he will crush your head, and you will strike his heel', Genesis 3:15) and, through the events described here, is now reaching its climax.

Notice how ancient prophecies are being fulfilled and circumstances arranged to fit into the divine timetable. Seemingly chance happenings on earth are, in fact, being orchestrated by a heavenly power. Things are coming to pass because God has decreed that the time is right (Galatians 4:4).

We need to recognize how God takes up into his eternal purposes ordinary, everyday people. They are remarkable for no other reason than the simplicity of their faith in God and their willingness to respond to what they sense he is asking of them. Truly God exalts the humble, as Mary declared in her song of praise (see Luke 1:52).

Marvel, too, as you see the supernatural breaking into the day-to-day pattern of events. These stories are full of heavenly surprises that cause amazement and wonder even now as we read them. Like Aslan in *The Lion, the Witch and the Wardrobe*, God is on the move and earth is shaken by his footsteps.

Above all, be aware that God will be speaking to you as you read and pray. Expect to encounter him as you meditate on scripture and reflect on its application to your life, for it is sacred history and alive with meaning and relevance for today.

*Tony Horsfall*

# Waiting

'But you, Bethlehem Ephrathah, though you are small among the clans of Judah, out of you will come for me one who will be ruler over Israel, whose origins are from of old, from ancient times.' Therefore Israel will be abandoned until the time when she who is in labour gives birth and the rest of his brothers return to join the Israelites. He will stand and shepherd his flock in the strength of the Lord, in the majesty of the name of the Lord his God. And they will live securely, for then his greatness will reach to the ends of the earth. And he will be our peace.

I remember as a young boy asking for my first pair of football boots for Christmas. I was so excited and couldn't wait for the big day to arrive. I can see them now—black with a white flash down each side and the latest rubber studs!

Waiting seems to be intrinsically linked to the Christmas season because there are so many preparations to be made and so many expectations of what it might bring. Feeling again a sense of waiting and longing, of yearning and hoping, is an essential spiritual dimension in celebrating the coming of the long-expected Messiah.

Prophets such as Micah reached beyond their immediate circumstances with bold predictions about one who would come as a true shepherd to care for the people of God. Amazingly, even the place of his birth is foretold. Such promises burned in the hearts of godly Israelites down the centuries.

People such as Simeon and Anna, for instance, looked for the consolation of Israel, waiting daily with great patience, anticipating the redemption of Jerusalem. So sure were they of the fulfilment of prophecy, they dared not leave the temple courts (see Luke 2:25–38).

What of our own waiting? Perhaps we have dreams yet to be realized, longings still to be satisfied, promises awaiting their fulfilment. Waiting for God is never easy, especially in a world that deliberately creates impatience within us.

## Reflection

*The Christmas season allows us to get in touch with our deepest desires and invites us to wait in faith. It gives us permission to hope, look forward and anticipate future blessing. Above all, it reminds us that, when the time is right, our faithful God will act.*

*TH*

# Greetings

In the sixth month of Elizabeth's pregnancy, God sent the angel Gabriel to Nazareth, a town in Galilee, to a virgin pledged to be married to a man named Joseph, a descendant of David. The virgin's name was Mary. The angel went to her and said, 'Greetings, you who are highly favoured! The Lord is with you.' Mary was greatly troubled at his words and wondered what kind of greeting this might be.

I expect that you have already been busy sending your Christmas greetings to family and friends. It is one aspect of this season that I enjoy, because keeping in touch and expressing appreciation are positive ways in which we can nurture our close relationships.

We enter Luke's account of the birth stories with the appearance of the angel Gabriel. The angel is sent by God to a specific place—Nazareth—a quiet country backwater without much to commend it and often scorned by others (John 1:46). Isn't it typical of God to begin his great work in the most unlikely of places?

The angel is also sent to a particular person—Mary—a young girl who is engaged to be married. Most scholars suggest that, according to normal Jewish custom and practice, she would probably have been in her mid teens. Again, there is nothing particularly remarkable about her, no human quality that would make her stand out or mark her as the obvious choice for a leading role in the unfolding drama of redemption. Again, it is characteristic of God to choose the 'weak' of this world to shame the 'strong'.

The angel begins with a special greeting, one full of encouragement. He announces to Mary that God is with her and is favoured by him. We would expect that such a positive blessing would lift her spirits but, instead, it troubles the young girl. Perhaps she senses there is more to come, the angel's blessing is a precursor of something greater that God is going to ask of her. Perhaps Mary was already aware in her own heart that God had a plan for her life and, in that moment, realizes what he has in mind for her is soon to be revealed.

### Prayer

*Lord, thank you that you chose ordinary people in ordinary places to be involved in your purposes.*

*TH*

# Child

But the angel said to her, 'Do not be afraid, Mary, you have found favour with God. You will conceive and give birth to a son, and you are to call him Jesus. He will be great and will be called the Son of the Most High. The Lord God will give him the throne of his father David, and he will reign over the house of Jacob forever; his kingdom will never end.' 'How will this be,' Mary asked the angel, 'since I am a virgin?'

Do you ever wonder where Mary was and what she was doing when she encountered the angel? Was it during a moment of frenzied domestic activity or a time of quiet contemplation? Was she taken completely by surprise or did she have an inkling that something unusual was about to happen? We cannot tell when or where the moment of annunciation took place. What we do know is that it must have shaken her to the core of her being.

To be told that you will have a child is one thing. To be told the child's gender and what to call him is even more surprising. To begin to realize that the child will somehow be integral to the outworking of the eternal purposes of God is even more staggering. I doubt that Mary could take in every detail of what the angel told her, let alone understand all the implications. She is hit, rather, by the impossibility of it as she knows herself to be a virgin and has no intention of giving herself to Joseph before they are married.

Her question, 'How can this be?' implies not so much unbelief and doubt, but puzzlement as to how these things could come about. She is, of course, seeing the situation from her own limited, earthly perspective—the viewpoint of a young girl growing up in the quiet backwater called Nazareth. The angel Gabriel comes from a different realm, he breathes the very atmosphere of heaven and is privy to the secrets of the Almighty. Not surprisingly, it takes a while for them to get on the same wavelength.

### Prayer

*Lord God, we ask that we, like Mary, may be open to your possibilities that are beyond anything we can imagine or ask for.*

TH

# Virgin

The angel answered, 'The Holy Spirit will come upon you, and the power of the Most High will overshadow you. So the holy one to be born will be called the Son of God. Even Elizabeth your relative is going to have a child in her old age, and she who was said to be barren is in her sixth month. For nothing is impossible with God.' 'I am the Lord's servant,' Mary answered. 'May it be to me as you have said.' Then the angel left her.

The virgin birth is one doctrine that some people find hard to accept. It is certainly not easy to understand and clearly contains an element of 'mystery', as even the apostle Paul concedes (1 Timothy 3:16), but it has always been considered central to orthodox Christianity.

The child to be born will be conceived by the power of the Holy Spirit—a direct creative act by God. At some point in time, the Spirit will 'come upon' her and gently 'overshadow' her. Mary's womb is to become the receptacle for the divine life and since there will be no human involvement in this supernatural process, it will guarantee that the child will be holy and without inherited sin. All this is possible because the almighty God is able to act outside the natural order of things.

To encourage Mary's faith, the angel informs her of what has happened to her cousin Elizabeth. In her case, the miracle is that she had been barren and was advanced in years. Now she too, is soon to have a child when it had seemed beyond the bounds of possibility.

Mary's response to what she is told is instructive. Whether she understands it fully or not, she accepts the angel's words and willingly offers herself to God so that his purpose can come to pass. Her reaction reflects the deeper attitude of her heart. Young as she is and humble as her circumstances may be, she is deeply devoted to God as a servant to her master. Gladly and joyfully she embraces God's will for her life, whatever it may mean.

## Reflection

*Someone has wisely said that surrender to God is in fact surrender to love. We need not be afraid of yielding ourselves and our future into his tender care. It may be scary, but it is safe.*

TH

LUKE 2:1–7 (NIV)

# Birth

In those days Caesar Augustus issued a decree that a census should be taken of the entire Roman world. (This was the first census that took place while Quirinius was governor of Syria.) And everyone went to their own towns to register. So Joseph also went up from the town of Nazareth in Galilee to Judea, to Bethlehem the town of David, because he belonged to the house and line of David. He went there to register with Mary, who was pledged to be married to him and was expecting a child. While they were there, the time came for the baby to be born, and she gave birth to her firstborn, a son. She wrapped him in cloths and placed him in a manger, because there was no room for them in the inn.

As I am a man, it goes without saying that I have never had the experience of giving birth. Although I am a father, I was not allowed to be present at the birth of either of my two children, so I have not even experienced the event at close quarters. However, I have it on good authority that it is quite an experience!

What I find remarkable about the birth of Jesus is that after the supernatural conception, it all happened so naturally. The embryo took the usual amount of time to form in the womb and Mary's body went through the normal changes associated with pregnancy. When the time came for the child to be born, I imagine that she had the fears and anxieties of any first-time mother, especially given the inconvenience and discomfort of an unexpected trip to Bethlehem and the unusual and possibly unhygienic surroundings in which she found herself. I guess, too, that it was an extremely painful yet amazingly beautiful experience.

Then, of course, the child has to be fed and cared for, clothed and cuddled like any other totally dependent newborn infant. All this is amazing when we remember that the baby was the Saviour of the world, the one destined to sit on David's throne and bring into being the kingdom of God. How humble God is to wrap himself in human flesh, how patient to let things take their natural time. How fully he has identified himself with us.

## Prayer

*Yea, Lord, we greet Thee,*
*born this happy morning!*

'O come, all ye faithful',
(John F. Wade, c. 1743)
TH

# Joy

And there were shepherds living out in the fields nearby, keeping watch over their flocks at night. An angel of the Lord appeared to them, and the glory of the Lord shone around them, and they were terrified. But the angel said to them, 'Do not be afraid. I bring you good news of great joy that will be for all the people. Today in the town of David a Saviour has been born to you; he is Christ the Lord. This will be a sign to you: you will find a baby wrapped in cloths and lying in a manger.'

It is to humble shepherds that the first announcement of the Saviour's birth is made. While in the town people are hurrying here and there, wrapped up in the importance of their own affairs and oblivious to eternal realities, outside on the hills, angelic activity is heralding the momentous event that has happened in their midst. For those who are aware of it, this is a day like no other—it is the day after the coming of the long-awaited Messiah.

How easy it is for us to become so engrossed in the business of living that we miss the most important things in life. The Christmas season is a good example. We can so fill our time with shopping, making preparations, seeing people, having a good time and, dare I say it, religious activities, that we have no time to be still and really consider what it is that we are celebrating. Sometimes it is good to step out of the 'town' and find a quiet spot 'in the fields' where we can reconnect with the true meaning of Christmas.

When we do this, we discover two important truths. First, this is an intensely personal matter. The Saviour is for all people, but he is given 'to you' in particular. He has come to save you from sin and bring you back to God.

Second, it is an extremely joyful occasion. The salvation of God is freely given and it is ours to be received by faith. That is good news indeed and, when we accept this gift from God, it liberates us from fear and brings a lasting joy to our hearts. That's what makes for a truly happy Christmas.

## Prayer

*Thanks be to God for his indescribable gift (2 Corinthians 9:15).*

TH

# Angels

Suddenly a great company of the heavenly host appeared with the angel, praising God and saying, 'Glory to God in the highest heaven, and on earth peace to those on whom his favour rests.' When the angels had left them and gone into heaven, the shepherds said to one another, 'Let's go to Bethlehem and see this thing that has happened, which the Lord has told us about.'

I'm told that choirs are very popular at the moment. There's something relaxing about joining with others and making music together and, in an increasingly stress-filled world, it's apparently becoming a sought-after leisure activity, especially among young professionals.

I don't think, though, that was quite the motive behind the formation of the angelic choir greeting the Saviour's birth. I'm sure angels are normally very busy and I imagine they can become stressed, but, really, they exist for one purpose only—to glorify God and do his will. For them, this celebration of the saving activity of God is something for which they were created and they take part in it with the utmost enthusiasm. We can only begin to imagine the beauty and harmony of the sound that filled the skies that night.

The angels' song is directed in two different directions. It is addressed heavenwards, first, giving glory to God for taking the initiative in salvation and having sent his Son into the world. For that, he deserves all the praise and honour and glory heaven and earth can give.

Second, it is directed earthwards, reminding us that the gift of the Saviour is an expression of his favour towards the world—he desires us to know his peace and live within his blessing, responding to him accordingly.

The shepherds enjoy the singing and no doubt marvel at the heavenly anthems, but their hearts are stirred not simply to admiration but also to action. They can stay no longer on the hillside. They must set off in search of the child and see for themselves the babe in the manger.

They are required, like everyone who hears the Christmas story, to make a journey of faith and take their first, faltering steps on the road of discipleship.

### Prayer

*Lord, may we not only hear the Christmas songs, but respond to their message.*

TH

# Wonder

So they hurried off and found Mary and Joseph, and the baby, who was lying in the manger. When they had seen him, they spread the word concerning what had been told them about this child, and all who heard it were amazed at what the shepherds said to them. But Mary treasured up all these things and pondered them in her heart. The shepherds returned, glorifying and praising God for all the things they had heard and seen, which were just as they had been told.

We have here two contrasting responses to the Christmas event. While the shepherds excitedly preach the word about the child, Mary quietly ponders in her heart the significance of it all.

Some people, like the shepherds, have, by personality, more of an extravert disposition. They live their lives in the outer world of people and events and activities. They like to be in groups, talk about what they are thinking and feeling and communicate easily what is going on inside them. God uses the naturally outgoing nature of the shepherds to communicate his message of salvation. They 'gossip the gospel' and all who meet them—friends and strangers alike—are amazed at the story they have to tell.

Other people, like Mary, have a more introvert disposition. They prefer to think things through, reflect deeply, and consider carefully what is going on around them. They enjoy time alone and are energized by stillness and silence. Thus, Mary chooses to take time to savour in her heart all that God has said to her and contemplate the deeper meaning behind what is going on around her. Tradition has it that her musings greatly influenced and informed the Gospel writers, especially Luke.

A balanced Christian life combines both reflection and action, contemplation and communication. We need to ponder the wonder of Christmas and take time to consider what God is saying to us through it, but we also need to share the life-giving and hope-inspiring message with others as often and as effectively as we can.

We may well find that one approach comes more easily and naturally to us, which is good, but we will be more rounded as people when we learn to do both.

### Prayer

*Lord, help us to pause and ponder, but also be bold enough to preach.*

TH

# Word

In the beginning was the Word, and the Word was with God, and the Word was God. He was with God in the beginning... The Word became flesh and made his dwelling among us. We have seen his glory, the glory of the one and only, who came from the Father, full of grace and truth.

Words are important to me because I earn my living by using them— in either my teaching or writing. I enjoy the challenge of finding the right words to express a thought and making complicated truths easier to understand. None of us can communicate fully without words —we all depend on them to share what we are thinking and feeling.

As we come to John's Gospel, we are enabled to stand back from the events of Christmas in order to consider the bigger picture. What is actually going on here? John's answer is that, through the birth of the Christ child, God is communicating with us, speaking to us in a language that we can understand. In a miraculous way, he has entered our world and become one of us. He has clothed himself in human flesh in order that we can see with our eyes what he is like and hear with our ears what he has to say. That is what we mean by incarnation—the invisible God becoming visible, God entering our world and becoming one with us, making himself accessible.

The writer to the Hebrews reminds us that God has spoken before, and in a variety of ways, but now he has spoken to us comprehensively and supremely in the coming of his Son (Hebrews 1:1–2). Jesus could be described as God's audiovisual aid. As we look at his life, we can see very clearly what God is like. Jesus is the exact word to describe God accurately and appropriately. As we listen to his teaching, we can hear what he has to say to us. There is no longer any room for confusion or misunderstanding. Eternal truth is made simple because the Word embodies it.

Petersen's telling paraphrase sums it up beautifully: 'The Word became flesh and blood and moved into the neighbourhood' (John 1:14, THE MESSAGE). That's it exactly—God as accessible, touchable, readable, understandable.

## Reflection

*'This is my Son, whom I love. Listen to him!' (Mark 9:7).*

TH

JOHN 1:3–9 (NIV)

# Light

Through him all things were made; without him nothing was made that has been made. In him was life, and that life was the light of men. The light shines in the darkness, but the darkness has not understood it. There came a man who was sent from God; his name was John. He came as a witness to testify concerning that light, so that through him all might believe. He himself was not the light; he came only as a witness to the light. The true light that gives light to every man was coming into the world.

It has recently become a custom in Britain for people to light up their houses at Christmas time—not just on the inside, but on the outside, too. Indeed, some families spend large sums of money decorating their homes with various seasonal lights—reindeers, Santas, stars and so on—and then collect money for charity from admiring passers-by.

In the northern hemisphere, the darkness of winter provides a symbolic backdrop to one of the 'bigger picture' aspects of Christmas. The birth of the Saviour is equated by John to the coming of light into a world darkened by sin and despair. As the 'light of the world' (John 8:12), the Christ child shines into our personal darkness to bring both revelation and illumination.

As the true light, Jesus provides an accurate revelation of God. The word 'true' suggests that there are 'false' representations of God around in the world and warns us of the danger of being led astray by them. It is important to hold a correct understanding of God in our minds, for how we conceive of God determines how we relate to him. Jesus has given us the authentic representation of what God is like, against which all other images must be measured.

Jesus also gives us spiritual illumination. It is as if the light is switched on inside our darkened minds and the truth that previously we did not know or could not understand suddenly dawns on us. Now we can see it, now we can understand. We have been enlightened—the light has entered into our minds and our hearts. We are no longer spiritually blind, but now we can see. The eyes of our hearts have been opened.

## Prayer

*Lighten our darkness,*
*we beseech Thee, O Lord.*

The Book of Common Prayer

*TH*

# Grace

John testifies concerning him. He cries out, saying, 'This was he of whom I said, "He who comes after me has surpassed me because he was before me."' From the fullness of his grace we have all received one blessing after another. For the law was given through Moses; grace and truth came through Jesus Christ. No one has ever seen God, but God the One and Only, who is at the Father's side, has made him known.

As the year draws to its close, we consider one final 'bigger picture' thought concerning the incarnation. In the person of Christ, God is speaking to us and his coming has brought light into the world. Now we see that the overarching reason for his appearance as a man is that we may receive his grace and experience God's blessing in our lives.

Grace is one of those words that is overused and underappreciated. It describes the loving activity of God towards us even though we are undeserving. It reminds us that we are loved unconditionally, unreservedly and unendingly.

The coming of Jesus inaugurates a new way of relating to God. It is not on the basis of the law, but on the basis of grace. Under the old covenant, represented by Moses, people sought to draw near to God on the basis of keeping laws—that is, by their own righteousness. As none of us can ever keep the law fully, that way of relating was doomed to failure. Indeed, its purpose was to show us that we cannot do it by ourselves, we need God's help.

Now we are to relate to God through Jesus. He came to fulfil the law on our behalf and give us the gift of his own righteousness. We can be made acceptable to God through his saving work on the cross. He was born to die and his death opens up for us the way of grace—coming to God trusting in his righteousness, not our own.

This grace is available in endless supply. It is available to us today in all its fullness. We can come back for more and come yet again and it will never be exhausted.

## Prayer

*Praise you, Lord, that you grant us grace to cover the mistakes and regrets of the year that is past and grace to strengthen us for what lies ahead.*

TH

# The BRF
## Magazine

# Richard Fisher writes...

Do you ever get bored with the Bible? It may sound a sacrilegious question to ask but, if we're honest (as we surely can be before God), we all sometimes need some extra motivation to help us over the dry patches and reignite our enthusiasm for reading. Well, this issue of the *BRF Magazine* is full of ideas to spark a new approach to exploring the Bible—one of BRF's core ministries.

First, Lisa Cherrett suggests some ways in which you can revitalize familiar parts of the scriptures and use them to launch into areas that you might not have explored so thoroughly before. Martyn Payne also offers some imaginative methods of refreshing well-known passages, in order to present them to children who may be hearing them for the first time. Along with other members of the *Barnabas* ministry team, Martyn works to bring the Bible to life for under-11s in churches and schools and is brimming with ideas for new approaches to old stories.

Naomi Starkey's recommendations in this issue, *Pilgrim's Way* by David Winter and *Twenty Questions Jesus Asked* by Elizabeth Rundle, are both by writers who have many years' experience of helping others to explore the Bible. Both bring fresh insights into some of the greatest passages of scripture, encouraging a genuine engagement with the word of God.

As you probably know, BRF publishes a new book especially for Advent and Lent each year. The stories of Jesus' birth and death are among the most familiar in the Bible, yet each of our authors brings their own unique approach to the subject matter. Michael Mitton, who has written our 2008 Advent book, is no exception: you'll find an extract from *A Handful of Light* on pages 144–147.

Finally, for a fun way into Bible exploration, turn to pages 150–153, where you'll find just a sample of the 80 crosswords in *Three Down, Nine Across* by John Capon. These puzzles range far and wide into the world of the Bible: if you manage to finish them all, you will have achieved quite a feat of discovery!

As Lisa Cherrett says, there are 'new and old treasures' to be found in the Bible. Why not go searching for a few of them with BRF?

*Richard Fisher, Chief Executive*

# Treasures from the storeroom

*Lisa Cherrett*

We all know the feeling: the Bible is a big book—indeed, a collection of books—and it can be overwhelming to think of delving into parts of it that we've never read before. I remember, as a young Christian, peeping into the book of Isaiah and hurriedly turning back to more familiar territory, thinking 'What was that all about?' So we stick with the bits we know, perhaps the Psalms and the Gospels, reading the same passages many times and neglecting the bulk of the collection.

Many of us would like to explore further, or at least find fresh nourishment in well-thumbed pages of the Bible. How can it be done?

One way to refresh our understanding of familiar passages is to read them in a translation (or paraphrase) different from the one we use most often. One of my major weaknesses as a Christian is fear, so perhaps it's not surprising that my favourite psalm is Psalm 91. I read it over and over again during a time of great stress and anxiety in my teenage years. When my spiritual director recently asked me to meditate on it, I wondered if I would really find anything new. So I decided to try THE MESSAGE, Eugene Peterson's contemporary paraphrase. As I reached verse 9 ('God's your refuge, the High God your very own home') my picture of 'refuge' changed completely.

Previously I'd imagined a grey cave in a rocky hillside, a 'make-do' place in which to take temporary shelter before heading out into the storm again. Now, as I meditated, the image in my mind became a castle with a heavy wooden door, and inside was a warm, brightly lit space with walls decorated in the same colour as my living room at home—a dwelling place, not a bolt-hole.

Even comparing a passage in two more exact translations can bring new light to our understanding. Take 1 Corinthians 13, Paul's famous chapter on love. Verse 5 in the NIV says, '… it is not self-seeking, it is not easily angered, it keeps no record of wrongs', while the NRSV translates, 'It does not insist on its own way; it is not irritable or resentful'. We might recognize our own less-than-loving behaviour easily in one of these descriptions but not in the other. Then, verse 10 says, '…when perfection comes, the imperfect disappears' (NIV) or '… when the complete comes, the partial will come to an end' (NRSV). In this case, the NRSV illuminates the fact that, in the Bible, 'perfection' usually means 'completeness' rather than 'moral purity'.

Even the best-known verses, then, can be given new life when seen from a different angle.

But how can we move on from those well-known passages of the Bible to open up new areas of study? A concordance is a useful tool for this purpose—a book that shows every word (at least, every major word) in the Bible and lists every passage containing that word. There are, of course, online concordances that allow you to search particular key words, as well as Bible references (see www.biblegateway.com).

It's interesting, for example, to take Psalm 23 as a launchpad and look for the word 'shepherd' in your concordance. You will probably soon notice a whole chapter elsewhere in the Old Testament that has several references to shepherds: Ezekiel 34. Here, in this otherwise rather difficult and obscure prophetic book, is an even more complete picture of what it means to say, 'The Lord is my

*Take Psalm 23 as a launchpad*

shepherd'. A little further down the concordance's list of references, John 10 stands out—the passage in which Jesus describes himself as the good shepherd, echoing the message of Ezekiel 34. So, working out from the most celebrated psalm of them all, we can discover why it was so important for Jesus to identify himself in this way, taking up an image that was central to the Old Testament prophets' understanding of God.

Simply looking at the length of the reference lists under certain words of the Bible in a concordance can be thought-provoking. The word 'faith', for instance, appears far more often in the New Testament than in the Old, whereas 'faithfulness' is more common in the Old than the New. What does this suggest? Perhaps that faith is a gift which became widely available only with the coming of Jesus, while the faithfulness of God himself has been established ever since he first revealed himself to his people?

Many people find reading the Old Testament a more daunting prospect than reading the New. We may even think that the Old Testament is not as relevant to us as Christians. Yet the New Testament writers pepper their work with quotations from the Old, and this can be a helpful aid for us if we want to venture further into the Hebrew Scriptures to see what they have to say to us.

Of the four Gospel writers, Matthew and Mark use the most Old Testament quotations, often to show how Jesus fulfilled messianic prophecies. The apostle Paul also quotes extensively, to link up his 'new' theological arguments with the knowledge of God revealed by others before him.

Some Bibles include footnotes that show the Old Testament origin of these biblical quotations in the Gospels and New Testament letters. For example, Mark 12: 30–31 tells us which of the commandments Jesus considered to be the most important and second most important: 'Love the Lord your God with all your heart and with all your soul and with all your mind and with all your strength' and 'Love your neighbour as yourself'. The footnotes in the NIV direct us to Deuteronomy 6:4–5 and Leviticus 19:18 respectively, both of which are significant but less well-known parts of the Bible. If you come across a similar cross-reference while reading a familiar passage, why not look it up? Then, to break new ground, read not only the quoted verse but also the few verses before and after it, or even the whole chapter.

Finally, of course, it is helpful to read books and commentaries that lead us deeper into our study of the Bible. There are at least two books available from BRF that take very well-known passages of scripture as their starting point. *A Fruitful Life* by Tony Horsfall is a close study of John 15—the chapter about Jesus as the vine—but quotes various Bible references along the way, showing how the lessons we can learn from the vine fit in with other important teachings in the Christian faith. *Living and Praying the Lord's Prayer,* by former *New Daylight* contributor Peter Graves, takes another familiar (perhaps overfamiliar) passage and recommends different parts of the Bible to study alongside, to open up the prayer further.

Jesus said, 'Every student of the Scriptures who becomes a disciple in the kingdom of heaven is like someone who brings out new and old treasures from the storeroom' (Matthew 13:52, CEV). It's good to have a stock of 'old treasures' from the Bible that we can call to mind at any time, to bring comfort and encouragement when necessary. It may be even better to see those well-loved gems as an investment that can help to build a store of new riches, just waiting to be found in scripture.

*Lisa Cherrett is BRF's Project Editor and Managing Editor for the Bible reading notes.*

*To order copies of* A Fruitful Life *or* Living and Praying the Lord's Prayer, *please turn to the order form on page 159.*

# The Editor recommends

*Naomi Starkey*

While summer holidays are still relatively fresh in our minds, it is worth pausing to ponder whether we are the sort who like going on organized tours, with well-planned itineraries and air-conditioned coaches or whether we prefer to make our own plans and find our own paths, with no more than a map and a couple of guidebooks in hand? Knowing our preferences and working with them (and sometimes against, just for a change) can help when it comes to Bible reading.

As we explore the Bible, we may prefer having passages chosen for us, along the lines of the 'daily readings' approach or we may like to strike off on our own, gaining insights along the way from sermons, home group discussions or helpful books. Two new BRF titles between them manage to offer both these approaches: *Pilgrim's Way* by David Winter and *Twenty Questions Jesus Asked* by Elizabeth Rundle.

David Winter's latest book draws in part on his extensive experience of writing daily reading notes for *New Daylight*. Subtitled 'Journeying through the year with the Bible', it is for all those who would like to get to know the Bible better, but don't know quite how to start. In fact, they would prefer some kind of tour guide to show them where to go.

David has selected 366 passages from both Old and New Testaments, one for every day including leap years, choosing well-known and loved passages, and also a wide selection of less familiar verses. Each Bible reading is linked to some explanatory comment and concludes with a final thought to lead into reflection and prayer. The readings are themselves grouped into themes, linked to the seasons of the calendar and of the Christian year.

*Pilgrim's Way* could prove to be a helpful gift for somebody you know who is relatively new to Bible reading. They may, for example, want to get better acquainted with a passage they remember from a recent wedding or funeral, but don't know how to go about finding it or don't understand what it is really saying. David's comment on each selection of verses is helpfully clear, even for those with limited Bible knowledge, and the book also includes an index of all references covered, to help with tracking down particular verses.

David Winter is one of the UK's most popular and long-established Christian writers and broadcasters. He has written many other books, including *Journey to Jerusalem* and *With Jesus in the Upper Room*, and *The Nation's Favourite Prayers*. He is also well known as a regular contributor to BBC Radio Four's *Thought for the Day*.

If, on the other hand, we're not so bothered about having the help of a Bible 'tour guide', we will probably enjoy spending time with Elizabeth Rundle's *Twenty Questions Jesus Asked*. Taking the Gospel accounts, this book focuses on the three short years of Jesus' ministry and, in particular, the questions he put to people, questions that were often life-changing in some way.

The book's challenge comes as we are then asked to imagine how we would respond if Jesus asked us one of those questions: 'What do you want? Why are you so afraid? Do you believe this? Who do you say I am?' and so on. It is not a case of knowing the 'right' answer but, as we reflect on the questions for ourselves, we may well find ourselves surprised and challenged, our hearts touched and our faith deepened. *Twenty Questions Jesus Asked* is warmly endorsed by Margaret Silf, who describes how it 'takes us right to Jesus' side, to hear the questions he has for *us*, and to reflect on our own responses'.

To use the holiday analogy one last time, reading this book is like a conversation we might strike up in a café with a fellow traveller. They could point out places we have never thought of visiting, views we have not seen, food we have not tasted. We come away refreshed and full of ideas for further exploration!

Elizabeth Rundle has many years' experience of helping people connect with God through scripture. She has contributed to *Day by Day with God* notes and has also written over a dozen books of Bible reflections, broadcast on local and national radio, and prepared scripts for television 'epilogue' slots.

It is arguable that exploring the Bible can actually prove as much of an adventure as criss-crossing the globe. Travel is commonly held to be life-enhancing and mind-broadening. In the same way, the longer we spend with the scriptures, the more we are moved to question previous assumptions, to think more deeply about what we have taken for granted. In so doing, we find that we are being changed, moulded by the Spirit day by day into the likeness of our heavenly Father.

*To order a copy of any of the BRF books mentioned here, please turn to the order form on page 159.*

# An extract from
# *A Handful of Light*

*A Handful of Light* is BRF's Advent book for 2008. Taking the theme of 'hope' and interweaving it with the themes of light and darkness found throughout the Bible, Michael Mitton has written readings for every day of the season, from 1 December to 6 January, the feast of the Epiphany. The book is for all those who want to reflect on how the yearning for 'something more' buried in every human heart connects with the hope of salvation manifested in the baby born in the stable. The following extract is the reading for 6 December.

## The Real Absence of God

*My God, my God, why have you forsaken me? Why are you so far from helping me, from the words of my groaning? O my God, I cry by day, but you do not answer; and by night, but find no rest. (Psalm 22:1–2)*

The season of Advent is traditionally a time when we think about the coming of God to earth. This is what the word 'advent' literally means. It comes from the Latin *advenio*, meaning 'to come to, arrive', and can also be used to mean 'to come near, to happen, to break out'. It's all about God breaking out of heaven at a particular time and coming to earth in the person of Jesus, and soon we shall be getting into those stories. Before we do that, we shall be looking at that uncomfortable experience in life when God does not seem to be on his way at all. In fact, if anything, it feels as if he has hurried back to heaven and locked the door with no intention of returning.

There is so much that is comforting about the Psalms. You read them and realize they were written by people who felt wonderfully free not only to offer lavish praise to the God they loved so much, but also to ask the most penetrating questions of him and even to shake their fists at him in anguish and anger. Today's Psalm is one that is very well known as it was quoted by Jesus on the cross (Matthew 27:46). But we are not going to think about Jesus on the cross today, because, significant though it is that he used this Psalm, these verses also have meaning for ordinary mortals going about their earthly lives.

In the introductory note in the original Hebrew text we are told that this is a Psalm written by David. The title of this Psalm is 'Plea for Deliverance from Suffering and Hostility'. It is written 'To the leader' and is to be sung to the tune of 'The Deer of the Dawn'. There is something very endearing about David. On the one hand he was the stuff real heroes are made of: a fantastic warrior, a great leader, a handsome man and a wise ruler. On the other hand he was also very flawed, seen not least in his fatal attraction to the beautiful Bathsheba (fatal, that is, not for David, but for Uriah, the unfortunate husband of Bathsheba for whom David arranged an untimely death. See 2 Samuel 11 for the full story). The writers of the life of David don't try to hide his mistakes from us, and similarly the compilers of the Psalms don't hide those Psalms that speak of human mistakes and anguish.

We don't know for certain who wrote this Psalm, but if it wasn't by David, it was by someone who was quite happy to attribute it to him and who was happy for us to know that David, although he was a great man of faith, had his times when God seemed uncomfortably distant.

*There are times when God feels close and other times when he seems distant*

The presence and absence of God is something that has always puzzled people. Trying to describe what it means to 'feel God close' takes a bit of doing, and there is nothing to verify experience in this way. Essentially it happens in the world of feelings and is a kind of intuition. Whatever it is, most people of faith will testify to the fact that there are times when God feels close and other times when he seems distant. Most of us can accept this, but it gets difficult when he appears distant at those times when we most need him to be close.

I suspect the context of this Psalm was just one such occasion. Here is David (or another person of faith, if it's not him) needing God to be close at an important time in his life, and instead it feels as if God has completely forsaken him and is so far away that he can no longer save him and is unable to hear the groans uttered by this desperate man. He cries out day and night, but all he gets is a cold comfort from heaven. Although he could really do with help, it seems that God is busy doing other things.

Some churches talk about the 'Real Presence' of God in the sacrament of Communion. But even in devout services of Holy Communion where he is meant to be so close, God can seem a million miles away. The writer Frederick Buechner describes this dilemma:

*The world hides God from us, or we hide ourselves from God, or for reasons of his own, God hides himself from us, but however you account for it, he is often more conspicuous by his absence than by his presence, and his absence is much of what we labour under and are heavy laden by. Just as sacramental theology speaks of a doctrine of the Real Presence, maybe it should speak also of a doctrine of the Real Absence because absence can be sacramental too, a door left open, a chamber of the heart kept ready and waiting.*

For me there is real hope in these words: 'Absence can be sacramental too.' I like the feel of that, but what does it actually mean? I was taught that a sacrament is an 'outward visible sign of an inward and spiritual grace' (not the easiest of concepts to understand at the best of times). If that is the case, then what kind of 'inward and spiritual grace' is signified by the sense of God's absence? If God feels absent to me, my first conclusion is that at best he is not interested and at worst he doesn't exist. Maybe, as ever, I need to look a bit closer at this apparent conundrum. I could go down the path of 'well, you can't rely on your feelings, you must simply believe the facts', which is all very well, but the fact is that I do actually need to feel that God is close at important times, just as I need my friends and family close. So what is this 'inward and spiritual grace' of absence? You are probably reading this thinking, 'Any minute now he will tell us, like that scene at the end of those *Poirot* films, where David Suchet as Poirot spreads out the facts and the sequence of events and then solves the mystery.' Would that I were the spiritual equivalent of Hercule Poirot! But no, I don't know the answers. I am simply someone like you, and someone like David, and we all have our times of crying out in pain and frustration 'My God, why have you forsaken me...?'

Do you see what is happening as we explore this theme? If there were 'Seven easy steps to discovering the presence of God in times of desolation', I would give them to you and no doubt you might be very impressed, and would try them out, probably on your own. But David made no attempt to take this approach, because he knew this was not the way of solving the problem. What is happening to us today as we wrestle with the presence/absence of God issue is that we are getting closer to one another. Rather than my

*Absence can be sacramental too*

telling you, it has now become a matter of 'us'. This is a question not for individuals but for the faith community, and it is one that actually builds community. If you start talking with someone else about your struggle with the apparent absence of God, and they say 'I have that experience, too', you will probably feel like hugging them! In a few moments you will be likely to feel really quite close to them—here is a friend who shares the same struggles. In time you find there are actually quite a few of you, including the odd person who writes books like this one you are reading, and kings in ancient times who wrote Psalms. All sorts of people have this problem. As we share openly together we sense there is someone listening to our conversation. Here is my paraphrase of John 20:19 to try to help explain this:

*Before long the risen Jesus will make his presence felt*

*On that day, when it was dark and the disciples were huddled together feeling lost and afraid and desperately missing their Lord, they suddenly discovered Jesus was with them and, standing right in the middle of them, he said to them 'My peace is with you', and it was.*

There will be times when we long for the advent, the coming of Jesus, especially when life is diffi-cult, and there will be times when we encounter not the presence, but the unwelcome absence of God. Those are the times to do what David did, which was not to hide away on his own, but to talk about it to the apparently distant God, and also talk to others, to share experience, to feel human warmth and contact. It is most likely that before long the risen Jesus will make his presence felt. To force it or hurry it will mean that you will miss his personal word of peace for your soul.

## Reflection
As your reflect on your life, can you see patterns or seasons when God feels close and when he feels absent? What has helped you regain a sense of his presence? If he feels absent at the moment, is there someone with whom you can share this experience?

## Prayer

*Lord, for the times when you are close, thank you. For the times when you are absent, lead me to those places where you can surprise me with your presence and bring me your word of peace.*

*To order a copy of this book, please turn to the order form on page 159.*

# Exploring Bible stories with children

*Martyn Payne*

**Many of the Bible stories that we use in our children's group will be very familiar to us. We may even have tackled these stories several times over the years. Unless we as leaders fall in love with the stories again each time, how can we expect the children to wonder and explore the story with enthusiasm and discover something fresh in them for themselves? What follows are ten ways in which you can keep your own Bible reading alive in preparation for your work with the children's groups committed to your care.**

No particular equipment is needed, just the Bible. Oh, and a willingness to use your imagination and see things differently! Perhaps this might mean spending longer just reading the story as of first importance, as opposed to spending time researching a new game, a clever craft or a complicated quiz.

## Imagine who was there

Think through who else was there at the time of the story but who is not mentioned in the text. Wonder about how the story looked and sounded from this person's point of view—for example, one of the guests at Mathew's meal for Jesus (Matthew 9:10), the prodigal son's mother, or Goliath's shield carrier.

## Ask about something puzzling

Work out at least one question to

do with the story, to which you definitely do not know the answer! For example:

- I wonder what Zacchæus did after Jesus left Jericho?
- I wonder how Mary managed to buy such expensive perfume to anoint Jesus' feet?
- I wonder what Noah's daughters-in-law did while on the ark?

## Cross-question the people

Imagine yourself being among the onlookers when the story takes place. What questions would you like to ask of the people who were there at the time? For example:

- Why can Pharaoh's priests copy-cat all your miracles, Moses?
- Why were you taken in at the wedding, Jacob?

- How did you know that Jesus was the Messiah when he came to be baptized by you, John?

## Hear the story

Read the story aloud to yourself a few times. Imagine the impact this would have had on the first-century listeners, who would have heard this story rather than reading it quietly to themselves as we do today.

## Place the story

Look at what story comes after and what story comes before the one you are reading. The writers put their stories together carefully and often with a definite purpose in the order. Can you see a reason why this story is where it is in the book?

## Take it personally

Imagine that this story is being told especially to you. Pause after each line and ask, 'I wonder why I need to read this story today? I wonder why I am being reminded of it at this precise moment in my life?'

## Translate the story

Put each line of the story into your own words, expanding or contracting the information and the language to fit your normal everyday vocabulary. In other words, imagine you are a 'translator' creating your own British MESSAGE version of the story.

## Retell the story

After a couple of readings, close the Bible and then tell the story out loud to yourself again. Note which parts have stayed most strongly with you and which parts you feel you needed to emphasize. Which parts of the story did you forget? Is there a reason, do you think?

## Make 'senses' of the story

Read through the story carefully and think what sounds, tastes and smells are involved. Visualize the story and take careful note of what you can see and touch. In other words, create the story in your imagination as a 3D film, in which all the five senses play a part.

## Rework the story

Turn the story into different styles of writing in your imagination. What would the story be like if it were written as a news report, a poem, a play, a diary entry, a letter to a friend, an instruction manual, or an entry in an encyclopedia? Look carefully at the feelings, the humour and the unrecorded responses of the people involved.

Here are just some of the ways in which we can come to the stories of the Bible afresh, letting the Holy Spirit take these timeless and inspired words and apply them first and foremost to our own lives, before we then explore them with our children.

*Martyn Payne's latest publication is* Footsteps to the Feast *(BRF, 2007), a book of activities for special times of the Christian year.*

# *Three Down Nine Across*

Here is the perfect book for everyone who loves crosswords and word puzzles. Originally published in *The Baptist Times*, these 80 Bible-based puzzles, compiled by John Capon, are an excellent resource for small group leaders wanting an imaginative approach to help people find their way round the scriptures. And they are a light-hearted way of reminding yourself of some wonderful Bible passages—and where to find them. All Bible quotations are taken from the New International Version.

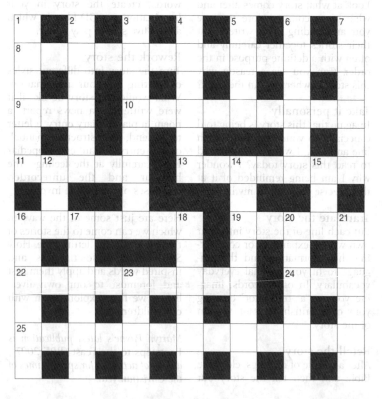

## Across

8   'Then Aaron and his sons and — — will be consecrated' (*Exodus 29:21*) (5,8)
9   'He lifted me out of the slimy — , out of the mud and mire' (*Psalm 40:2*) (3)
10  Such a person should be put to death (*Leviticus 20:27*) (9)
11  Chain of mountains (*Numbers 27:12*) (5)
13  'They are worse off at the — — they were at the beginning' (*2 Peter 2:20*) (3,4)
16  Descent (anag.) (7)
19  'But they all alike — to make excuses' (*Luke 14:18*) (5)
22  Reimbursement (*Luke 6:34*) (9)
24  Female sheep (*2 Samuel 12:4*) (3)
25  ' — — is too wonderful for me, too lofty for me to attain' (*Psalm 139:6*) (4,9)

## Down

1   Alcohol-induced oblivion (*Psalm 78:65*) (6)
2   'Three times I was — with rods' (*2 Corinthians 11:25*) (6)
3   Future outlook (*Proverbs 10:28*) (8)
4   It caused Joseph's brothers to journey to Egypt to buy grain (*Genesis 42:5*) (6)
5   See 15 Down
6   'You care for the land and water it; you — it abundantly' (*Psalm 65:9*) (6)
7   Son of Mehir and descendant of Judah (*1 Chronicles 4:11*) (6)
12  Car (anag.) (3)
14  Engage in warfare (*Isaiah 31:4*) (2,6)
15  'In the thirty-first year of — king of Judah, — became king of Israel' (*1 Kings 16:23*) (3,4)
16  Excessive strain or tension (*Jeremiah 19:9*) (6)
17  'The Son of Man will come at an hour when you do not — him' (*Luke 12:40*) (6)
18  'Very rarely will anyone — — a righteous man' (*Romans 5:7*) (3,3)
20  Avaricious (*1 Peter 5:2*) (6)
21  'Martha, Martha, you are worried and upset about many things, but only one thing is — ' (*Luke 10:41–42*) (6)
23  'For my — is easy and my burden is light' (*Matthew 11:30*) (4)

## Across

1    Under these Hagar put Ishmael to die *(Genesis 21:15)* (6)
4    Vantage point from which Moses saw the promised land before he died *(Deuteronomy 34:1)* (6)
7    'The Lord is compassionate and gracious, — to anger, abounding in love' *(Psalm 103:8)* (4)
8    'When he sees the wolf coming the hired hand — the sheep and runs away' *(John 10:12)* (8)
9    The world's first steam-worked public railway, — to Darlington (8)
13   It helped to provide the honey inside the carcass of the lion Samson killed *(Judges 14:8)* (3)
16   High Church (5-8)

17    Possessive pronoun (3)
19    Plotting (*Nehemiah 6:2*) (8)
24    'Lovers of — rather than lovers of God' (*2 Timothy 3:4*) (8)
25    Destroy by fire (*Deuteronomy 7:5*) (4)
26    'He who has been stealing must steal no longer, but must work, doing something — with his hands' (*Ephesians 4:28*) (6)
27    One of the colours of the riders' breastplates in John's vision (*Revelation 9:17*) (6)

## Down

1    'The father said to his servants, "Quick! Bring me the — robe and put it on him"' (*Luke 15:22*) (4)
2    Ghosts are (anag.) (9)
3    A small one can set a great forest on fire (*James 3:5*) (5)
4    Instrument used as accompaniment in some churches (5)
5    'A Levite, when he came to the place and saw him, passed by on the other — ' (*Luke 10:32*) (4)
6    Swiss illustrator of the Good News Bible, — Vallotton (5)
10    'In the — of Christ I glory, towering o'er the wrecks of time' (5)
11    Paul told Timothy that an overseer in the church must be able to do this (*1 Timothy 3:2*) (5)
12    Comes between Micah and Habakkuk (5)
13    Ill in a bug (anag.) (9)
14    'They saw what seemed to be tongues of fire that separated and came to rest on — of them' (*Acts 2:3*) (4)
15    Controversial artist best known for his Christ of St John of the Cross, Salvador — (4)
18    'Have nothing to do with godless myths and old wives' — ' (*1 Timothy 4:7*) (5)
20    Barbaric (*Jeremiah 6:23*) (5)
21    Adversary (*Luke 10:19*) (5)
22    The portion of his possessions that Zacchaeus told Jesus he would give to the poor (*Luke 19:8*) (4)
23    'Though your sins are like scarlet, they shall be as white as — ' (*Isaiah 1:18*) (4)

*To order a copy of this book, please turn to the order form on page 159. For the answers to these two crosswords, visit our website: www.brf.org.uk/product/9781841015477.htm*

New Daylight © BRF 2008

**The Bible Reading Fellowship**
15 The Chambers, Vineyard, Abingdon OX14 3FE
Tel: 01865 319700; Fax: 01865 319701
E-mail: enquiries@brf.org.uk; Website: www.brf.org.uk

ISBN 978 1 84101 478 4

Distributed in Australia by:
Willow Connection, PO Box 288, Brookvale, NSW 2100.
Tel: 02 9948 3957; Fax: 02 9948 8153;
E-mail: info@willowconnection.com.au
Available also from all good Christian bookshops in Australia.
For individual and group subscriptions in Australia:
Mrs Rosemary Morrall, PO Box W35, Wanniassa, ACT 2903.

Distributed in New Zealand by:
Scripture Union Wholesale, PO Box 760, Wellington
Tel: 04 385 0421; Fax: 04 384 3990; E-mail: suwholesale@clear.net.nz

Distributed in Canada by:
The Anglican Book Centre, 80 Hayden Street, Toronto, Ontario, M4Y 3G2
Tel: 001 416 924-1332; Fax: 001 416 924-2760;
E-mail: abc@anglicanbookcentre.com; Website: www.anglicanbookcentre.com

Publications distributed to more than 60 countries

**Acknowledgments**

Printed in Singapore by Craft Print International Ltd

BRF is a Christian charity committed to resourcing the spiritual journey of adults and children alike. For adults, BRF publishes Bible reading notes and books and offers an annual programme of quiet days and retreats. Under its children's imprint *Barnabas*, BRF publishes a wide range of books for those working with children under 11 in school, church and home. BRF's *Barnabas Ministry* team offers INSET sessions for primary teachers, training for children's leaders in church, quiet days, and a range of events to enable children themselves to engage with the Bible and its message.

We need your help if we are to make a real impact on the local church and community. In an increasingly secular world people need even more help with their Bible reading, their prayer and their discipleship. We can do something about this, but our resources are limited. With your help, if we all do a little, together we can make a huge difference.

## How can you help?

- You could support BRF's ministry with a donation or standing order (using the response form overleaf).

- You could consider making a bequest to BRF in your will, and so give lasting support to our work. (We have a leaflet available with more information about this, which can be requested using the form overleaf.)

- And, most important of all, you could support BRF with your prayers.

Whatever you can do or give, we thank you for your support.

*BRF – resourcing your spiritual journey*

# BRF MINISTRY APPEAL RESPONSE FORM

Name _____

Address _____

_____ Postcode _____

Telephone _____ Email _____

(tick as appropriate)

**Gift Aid Declaration**

❏ I am a UK taxpayer. I want BRF to treat as Gift Aid Donations all donations I make from 6 April 2000 until I notify you otherwise.

Signature _____ Date _____

❏ I would like to support BRF's ministry with a regular donation by standing order (please complete the Banker's Order below).

**Standing Order – Banker's Order**

To the Manager, Name of Bank/Building Society _____

Address _____

_____ Postcode _____

Sort Code _____ Account Name _____

Account No _____

Please pay Royal Bank of Scotland plc, Drummonds, 49 Charing Cross, London SW1A 2DX (Sort Code 16-00-38), for the account of BRF A/C No. 00774151

The sum of _____ pounds on ___ /___ /___ (insert date your standing order starts) and thereafter the same amount on the same day of each month until further notice.

Signature _____ Date _____

**Single donation**

❏ I enclose my cheque/credit card/Switch card details for a donation of
£5 £10 £25 £50 £100 £250 (other) £ _____ to support BRF's ministry

Credit/Switch card no. ❏❏❏❏❏❏❏❏❏❏❏❏❏❏❏❏❏❏❏

Expires ❏❏❏❏ Security code ❏❏❏ Issue no. of Switch card ❏❏❏❏

Signature _____ Date _____

(Where appropriate, on receipt of your donation, we will send you a Gift Aid form)

❏ Please send me information about making a bequest to BRF in my will.

**Please detach and send this completed form to:** Richard Fisher, BRF, 15 The Chambers, Vineyard, Abingdon OX14 3FE. BRF is a Registered Charity (No.233280)

ND0308

# BIBLE READING RESOURCES PACK

A pack of resources and ideas to help to promote Bible reading in your church is available from BRF. The pack, which will be of use at any time during the year, includes sample editions of the notes, magazine articles, leaflets about BRF Bible reading resources and much more. Unless you specify the month in which you would like the pack sent, we will send it immediately on receipt of your order. We greatly appreciate your donations towards the cost of producing the pack (without them we would not be able to make the pack available) and we welcome your comments about the contents of the pack and your ideas for future ones.

This coupon should be sent to:

BRF
15 The Chambers
Vineyard
Abingdon
OX14 3FE

Name _____

Address _____

_____

_____ Postcode _____

Telephone _____

Email _____

Please send me _____ Bible Reading Resources Pack(s)

Please send the pack now/ in _____ (month).

I enclose a donation for £ _____ towards the cost of the pack.

BRF is a Registered Charity

# SUBSCRIPTIONS

❏ Please send me a Bible reading resources pack to encourage Bible reading in my church
❏ I would like to take out a subscription myself (complete your name and address details only once)
❏ I would like to give a gift subscription (please complete both name and address sections below)

Your name _____

Your address _____

_____Postcode _____

Gift subscription name _____

Gift subscription address _____

_____Postcode _____

Please send *New Daylight* beginning with the January / May / September 2009 issue:   (delete as applicable)

| (please tick box) | UK | SURFACE | AIR MAIL |
|---|---|---|---|
| NEW DAYLIGHT | ❏ £13.35 | ❏ £14.55 | ❏ £16.65 |
| NEW DAYLIGHT 3-year sub | ❏ £30.00 | | |
| NEW DAYLIGHT DELUXE | ❏ £17.25 | ❏ £21.60 | ❏ £26.70 |

I would like to take out an annual subscription to *Quiet Spaces* beginning with the next available issue:

| (please tick box) | UK | SURFACE | AIR MAIL |
|---|---|---|---|
| QUIET SPACES | ❏ £16.95 | ❏ £18.45 | ❏ £20.85 |

Please complete the payment details below and send your coupon, with appropriate payment, to:
BRF, 15 The Chambers, Vineyard, Abingdon OX14 3FE.

Total enclosed £ _____ (cheques should be made payable to 'BRF')

**Payment by** cheque ❏ postal order ❏ Visa ❏ Mastercard ❏ Switch ❏

Card number: ⬚⬚⬚⬚⬚⬚⬚⬚⬚⬚⬚⬚⬚⬚⬚⬚⬚⬚⬚⬚

Expires: ⬚⬚⬚⬚   Security code ⬚⬚⬚   Issue no (Switch): ⬚⬚⬚⬚

Signature (essential if paying by credit/Switch card) _____

BRF is a Registered Charity

ND0308

# BRF PUBLICATIONS ORDER FORM

Please ensure that you complete and send off both sides of this order form.
Please send me the following book(s):

| | | Quantity | Price | Total |
|---|---|---|---|---|
| *Featured on inside cover:* | | | | |
| 247 6 | A Handful of Light (M. Mitton) | ___ | £7.99 | ___ |
| 594 1 | Make & Do Christmas Cards and Crib (J. Godfrey) | ___ | £5.99 | ___ |
| 595 8 | Make & Do Christmas Puppet Plays (J. Martin-Scott) | ___ | £12.99 | ___ |
| 593 4 | The Christmas Baby (S.A Wright) | ___ | £5.99 | ___ |
| 534 7 | Bethlehem Carols Unpacked (M. Payne/L. Moore) | ___ | £8.99 | ___ |
| *Featured in the BRF Magazine:* | | | | |
| 335 0 | A Fruitful Life (T. Horsfall) | ___ | £6.99 | ___ |
| 182 0 | Living and Praying the Lord's Prayer (P. Graves) | ___ | £6.99 | ___ |
| 529 3 | Pilgrim's Way (D. Winter) | ___ | £9.99 | ___ |
| 568 2 | Twenty Questions Jesus Asked (E. Rundle) | ___ | £6.99 | ___ |
| 485 2 | Journey to Jerusalem (D. Winter) | ___ | £7.99 | ___ |
| 324 4 | With Jesus in the Upper Room (D. Winter) | ___ | £6.99 | ___ |
| 464 7 | Footsteps to the Feast (M. Payne) | ___ | £8.99 | ___ |
| 547 7 | Three Down, Nine Across (J. Capon) | ___ | £6.99 | ___ |
| *Titles by New Daylight contributors:* | | | | |
| 565 1 | Crying for the Light (V. Zundel) | ___ | £5.99 | ___ |
| 402 8 | Marriage—Restoring Our Vision (D. Robertson) | ___ | £7.99 | ___ |
| 493 1 | Collaborative Ministry (D. Robertson) | ___ | £8.99 | ___ |
| 126 4 | Living the Gospel (Helen Julian) | ___ | £5.99 | ___ |
| 486 9 | When the Time Was Right (S. Rand) | ___ | £7.99 | ___ |
| 531 6 | When You Walk (A. Plass) | ___ | £9.99 | ___ |
| 505 9 | Blind Spots in the Bible (A. Plass) | ___ | £7.99 | ___ |
| 562 0 | Mentoring for Spiritual Growth (T. Horsfall) | ___ | £7.99 | ___ |
| *Recommended PBCs:* | | | | |
| 066 9 | PBC: Exodus (H.R. Page Jr) | ___ | £8.99 | ___ |
| 071 7 | PBC: Proverbs (E.B. Mellor) | ___ | £7.99 | ___ |
| 082 3 | PBC: Romans (J.D.G. Dunn) | ___ | £8.99 | ___ |
| 122 6 | PBC: 1 Corinthians (J. Murphy-O'Connor) | ___ | £7.99 | ___ |

| POSTAGE AND PACKING CHARGES | | | | |
|---|---|---|---|---|
| order value | UK | Europe | Surface | Air Mail |
| £7.00 & under | £1.25 | £3.00 | £3.50 | £5.50 |
| £7.01–£30.00 | £2.25 | £5.50 | £6.50 | £10.00 |
| Over £30.00 | free | prices on request | | |

Total cost of books £ ___
Donation £ ___
Postage and packing £ ___
TOTAL £ ___

See over for payment details. All prices are correct at time of going to press, are subject to the prevailing rate of VAT and may be subject to change without prior warning.

Please complete the payment details below and send with appropriate payment and completed order form to:

**BRF, 15 The Chambers, Vineyard,
Abingdon OX14 3FE**

Name _____

Address _____

_____

_____ Postcode _____

Telephone _____

Email _____

Total enclosed £ _____(cheques should be made payable to 'BRF')

Payment by cheque ❏ postal order ❏ Visa ❏ Mastercard ❏ Switch ❏

Card number: ☐☐☐☐☐☐☐☐☐☐☐☐☐☐☐☐☐☐☐

Expires: ☐☐☐☐  Security code ☐☐☐  Issue no (Switch): ☐☐☐☐

Signature (essential if paying by credit/Switch card) _____

❏ Please do not send me further information about BRF publications.

ALTERNATIVE WAYS TO ORDER

**Christian bookshops:** All good Christian bookshops stock BRF publications. For your nearest stockist, please contact BRF.

**Telephone:** The BRF office is open between 09.15 and 17.30.
To place your order, phone 01865 319700; fax 01865 319701.

**Web:** Visit www.brf.org.uk